What Kids Really

About

What Kids Really Want to Know About Sex

Telling Teenagers the Truth

Phillip Hodson

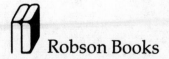

Robson Books

First published in Great Britain in 1993 by Robson
Books Ltd, Bolsover House, 5–6 Clipstone Street,
London W1P 7EB

Copyright © 1993 Phillip Hodson

The right of Phillip Hodson to be identified as author
of this work has been asserted by him in accordance
without the Copyright, Designs and Patents Act 1988

British Library Cataloguing in Publication Data
A catalogue record for this book is available from the
British Library

ISBN 0 86051 882 5

Photoset in North Wales by Derek Doyle &
Associates, Mold, Clwyd

Printed and bound in Great Britain by
Butler & Tanner Ltd, Frome and London

Contents

Acknowledgements

Some of the material in this book has previously appeared in *365 Ways To Have A Happy Sex-Life* by Phillip Hodson and Anne Hooper (Thorsons, 1990), and is reproduced by kind permission of the publishers. Other letters have been drawn from *Family Circle* and *TV Quick*, and I'm also grateful to the BBC for the use of letters received through my television programmes and *Fast Forward* Magazine. Linda Thompson and Anne Hooper have made invaluable suggestions throughout the editing phase of this book and Linda did hours of typing which is why it appeared in 1993 not 1994.

Preface

Ninety per cent of the letters in this book have been written by people in your age group. You may find some of them relate directly to you, some to your brothers and sisters, some to your friends and family. I've tried my best to give answers without bias. I think growing up is hard enough without having old people make fun of your feelings. The big advantage of this book is that it's embarrassment-free. You'll find nearly all the information you want just by reading it. But I hope afterwards you'll feel confident enough to talk to anyone without blushing – even your parents! PS: The last chapter contains letters from them, in case you wanted to teach them something.

Introduction: Preamble for Parents

'If 13-year-olds are too immature to understand the emotions of Shakespeare's 13-year-old Juliet, why are their teachers so afraid that they may get pregnant?' – Letter to *The Times*, June 1992.

For the past few years I've written columns for *Today*, *She* Magazine, *Family Circle*, *TV Quick*, *Fast Forward* and the *News of the World*, all of which have brought me a flood of letters. I've also had a huge postbag from my fifteen years of radio with LBC, plus television with *Problem Page* on TVS, *People Today* on BBC Daytime, BBC's *Going Live!*, and GMTV. I cannot claim to have answered every single letter sent in (that would be impossible – I have helpers) but I've certainly read everything received. The accumulated total is over 180,000 items of correspondence.

Many of these letters are from young people aged ten to twenty, especially those arising from that section of my *News of the World* column called 'PROBS – Growing Up Is Hard To Do'. From them I've been able to see many of the changes in young behaviour since the

1970s. This doesn't mean I can always keep up to speed
or move with the times – as my own children will be the
first to point out – but at least I've been able to notice
much of what's happened and try to react to new
situations and offer help when required.

The following pages show in great detail how today's
teens and pre-teens are trying to cope with sex in the
age of recession, soap opera and Aids. Some young
people want to go steady at ten. A decade ago, they
would have waited till they were fifteen. Girls of eleven
want to know how to french kiss. Boys of twelve want
to 'get off' with their girlfriends. In 1990, over 8,000 girls
under the age of consent had babies. That's two per
secondary school in England and Wales. Thousands
more had abortions. Some girls cannot discuss periods
with their mums. Many boys – who get no menstrual
education whatsoever – think periods are a type of
disease. To some, safe sex still means withdrawal. By
much of this I'm saddened but not surprised.

The point is we still don't really tell teenagers the
truth. Most of the letters in this book were not
published in magazine columns, for reasons of editorial
reticence. The same culture which exploits sex for cash,
persuading young people to ape their elders, remains
unwilling to answer the questions begged.

As adults, we remain uncomfortable with sex. The
English still think it's funny to call a situation comedy
Bottom, we get our knickers in a twist when women's
towels with wings are advertised on television, and
regard toe-sucking as a perversion not foreplay. My
contention is that by providing little straightforward,
snigger-free information for youngsters we create the
very problems we deplore. The fact is that countries
with the most open attitudes towards sex education and
contraceptive advice for young people, such as the

Netherlands, tend to have the lowest teenage pregnancy and abortion rates. (For the record, in the UK, we
have 70 pregnancies in every 1,000 teenage girls – and
on average 50 per cent of all sixteen-year-olds have had
sex. In sharp contrast Holland shows only *eight*
pregnancies in every 1,000 teenage girls with the
average age for first sex at seventeen-and-a-quarter.)
Parents who don't tell their young children the facts of
life, or shelter them from news programmes on
deviance and abuse, render them more vulnerable to
danger. An ignorant child is obviously an unprotected
child.

The child remains ignorant in school. In June 1992,
the National Children's Bureau published the results of
a detailed survey (*An Inquiry into Sex Education*) showing
that less than half the education authorities in England
and Wales ran properly monitored sex-education
classes. Barriers to progress included 'teacher dif-
fidence, especially among males', 'feelings of embarrassment and uncertainty', 'inhibitions among head
teachers and governors', 'worries about parental
disapproval' and 'lack of budget'. One health education
co-ordinator said: 'I have no budget ... and six books.'
Where education is offered, 'little attention is given to
attitudes and feelings'. In other words, it's no use
expecting the schools to cope if we as parents don't
supply those 'missing conversations'.

I recognize that many teenagers most need to discuss
sex at a stage in their lives when they least want to do
this with their parents. In 1991, a Health Education
Survey showed that while young women do approach
their mothers to discuss sex more frequently than do
men (66 per cent as opposed to 40 per cent), both rarely
approach their fathers (18 per cent for women, 27 per
cent for men). Peers are, as is often suspected, the

greatest source of sexual information (80 per cent), then teachers (at 13 per cent) and GPs (six per cent). However, that is not to let us off the hook. Surely we could make ourselves more approachable and better informed? It doesn't seem very clever to leave children to be instructed by playground seers. One seven-year-old girl was solemnly told that every time she had her period she would lose eight gallons of blood ... A boy, slightly older, announced to friends you can't get Aids if you wear a condom. When asked what that was he said: 'A rubber tube – you wear it on your finger.'

The least we can do is start conversations at home based on accurate knowledge. What's needed is 'much more information at a much earlier stage – such as nine. As well as the usual details of sexual intercourse and pregnancy, children should be taught how to handle falling in love, being *besotted*, relationships, feelings ...' (Frances Hudson of the Schoolgirl Mothers Unit, Bristol). Today's young people are both blunt and idealistic. This book aims to answer their questions honestly and openly. I hope it circulates in a few playgrounds. For some parents, it may prove an education. For some distressed and anxious teenagers, who may be having risky sex or abortions, it could be a lifeline. For others, it will offer reassurance in a world where childhood now seems to end almost before it's begun.

1

Love and Petting

As your teens start you naturally think about sex and close relationships because very powerful hormones are surging through your body. Equally strong messages are sent via TV and magazines showing you how great it can be to fall in love. As a result, girls and boys of nine or ten nowadays talk about 'going steady'. But true life is rarely as simple as stories. There is a whole group of problems to do with love and petting you may need help with – differences in age, teasing from friends, confusion over whether to go further, trouble with parents, ignorance of how to behave towards pushy people and liars, what to do and what NOT to do when your body says DO EVERYTHING.

Naughty but nice

I am twelve years old and have a fourteen-year-old boyfriend. Because he is so much older, he thinks I have

1

been through the same things as him. When I am at his house, he tries to feel me in unspeakable places. He is really nice but I don't know how I can keep going out with him. I can't tell my mum, because I don't know what she would say. Please help me! Glenys.

Answer

I'm sorry you can't tell your mum because it would be nice to have her on your side. What she would probably say is that loving someone does *not* mean always doing what they want. You've made it perfectly clear, in a sensible way, that you aren't comfortable with your boyfriend's behaviour. Loving you should mean that he won't force you. So ask him to be nicer still and keep his hands to himself.

Do I love him?

I really like a boy who I see quite often. When I think about him I get a tingly feeling all over and my legs, feet and arms seem cold without actually being cold. It's like what I get before Christmas Day or when you're nervous. My friend fancies him too but it's a secret between us. Do I really love him? I am only ten and so is he. Please help. Melanie.

Answer

People use the word love to mean different things. In the best sense, you love someone because you've had a good chance to get to know them. At present, it's probably more accurate to say you fancy this boy. He gives you a definite physical tingle of pleasure and a thrill of excitement. It might turn into love one day, but only when you discover whether he pleases your mind as well as your body. What if he tortures frogs? Or picks his nose? Or hates girls? Some of these things might just matter, yes?

Loneliness

I am thirteen years old and have a bit of a problem. There's a boy at school that I'm really attracted to and he knows I am, but he takes advantage of this to get money and other things from me. I don't know what to do because I fancy him so much and haven't got the heart to tell him to go away. Lonely Girl.

Answer

Well, he's got no heart or he wouldn't be cashing in on your loneliness. In a sad sort of way, you've been reduced to buying his attention. This tells me just how lonely you feel. It also tells me you don't know how to solve your problem. Please stop thinking you are worthless. If you feel inferior, that is because someone has been getting at you. (Maybe this bloke?) Or you blame all your loneliness on yourself. Anyone can get lonely by staying at home and becoming afraid to make new friends. Make the decision to circulate more. Look people in the eye. Smile more. Breathe in before you speak. Plan what you want to say. This will give you lots more confidence. Enough confidence to tell this guy he's cheap at any price.

What's what

Please please help me. Recently a boy asked me out and I did not know whether to say yes or no. I said yes, but the problem is I don't know what 'going out' means. Does it mean I will go out with him to a place or does it mean we just love each other from now on? Please help.

I'm ten. I do not see how anybody at my age could go to places with anybody when they are so young. Puzzled At Ten.

Answer

And you're right. Going out with/going with usually means you've become best friends with someone of the opposite sex. So no one is expecting you to announce you're off to New York for a weekend alone with your fella. However, don't let anyone push you around. If you keep saying yes before you know what the question means you could end up in all sorts of pickles, couldn't you?

How to break up

Please help – I'm in a terrible dilemma and you are the only person I trust. Back in July, I started going out with a girl. And so far we have been having a perfectly good relationship. However, where I go to school is a girl in the year below me who fancies me a lot and the problem is the feeling is mutual. She knows this but unfortunately my present girlfriend doesn't. I really want to start going steady with this new girl but cannot bring myself to tell my present girlfriend. This problem is driving me crazy. I really do want it solved. Please help. Confused Fourteen-year-old Boy.

Answer

What stops you speaking up is a fear of confrontation. Perhaps you think your present girlfriend will scream and shout or cry? But we can't go through life avoiding emotion. However difficult it seems, just tell yourself everyone is entitled to break up and move on provided they do it honestly. Choose a time to tell your friend face-to-face that your feelings are not the same as they were so you can no longer go out with her.

In a fix

I am just twelve years old and at my senior school. Ever since I've been there I haven't been able to take my eyes off this girl who is in my class nor have I been able to bring myself to ask her out. Recently, my problem has become worse as another girl has asked me out and I have gone with her even though I do not in any way find her attractive. I can't 'dump' her because I know it would break her heart but at the same time I really fancy the other girl ... Please help me, I don't know what to do. Greg.

Answer

Of the three people involved in this, two are unhappy. You want to go out with someone else. Your present girlfriend must know you feel half-hearted about her. It's unkind to leave things this way. It isn't 'dumping' someone to say things are over. It's called 'ending'. If you do it nicely, people recover. 'Dumping' happens when you don't tell them it's finished but let them find out for themselves. You have to learn to face your feelings. Tell both girls the truth. If you don't, you could even end up married one day to someone you 'do not in any way find attractive' just to avoid a row. And that would really be tough.

How to move on

I've come to England from California for two and a half months. After we go back, we're moving to St Louis, Missouri. I've been going out with this guy for four weeks. We really like each other but I think he expects our relationship to go on after I move to the States. But I'm ready to move on. How do I tell him in such a way that he knows I still care? I don't want to hurt him. From Nervous.

Answer

Since you can't give him what he wants, you can't prevent him from feeling disappointed. However, you could say some nice things too – 'I like you – it's geography that's mainly breaking us up.' Show him on the atlas how many squillions of miles away it is to St Louis and agree to write to him.

The boy next door

I fancy the boy who lives next door to me but I don't know his name or anything. He only comes home at weekends. He's about thirteen or fourteen and I am eleven but I can't stop thinking about him. I keep looking out of the window everyday for him. I want to ask him on a date but I don't know how to. From Gaby.

Answer

Gaby, why don't you throw a ball over the garden fence one Saturday, knock on your neighbour's door and ask if you can have your ball back? Then say who you are. When you notice this boy in his garden later, lose your ball again and see if you two can get talking?

Too immature

I've been in love with this girl ever since the first year of secondary school. But each time I ask her out she says no. She says I'm immature and need to grow up. I've tried growing up and being sensible at school but she still says no! I love her to pieces. Please could you tell me what to do? Thanks, Anon.

Answer

Obviously, you can't 'instantly grow up' and it's true that boys on average do develop a year or so later than girls. But the most difficult part of growing up is learning to accept that sometimes no means no. The funny thing is – maybe this girl would like you a bit more if you backed off?

Boy Dreams

I'm eleven and madly in love with this boy in my class. The problem is I'm quite a shy girl when I'm around boys of my own age. I had this dream last night about this boy kissing me. What does this mean? When I see him I feel like I want to kiss him. Louise.

Answer

The dream means two things. First, that you are thinking about this boy. Second that your body is growing up and making you have dreams you would not have had five years ago (when you were probably into My Little Pony). What it doesn't mean is that you have to go out and kiss him.

Wants more than just friends

I'm in love with this boy. We're good friends and he's a year younger than me. I don't want to spoil our friendship. He's been out with some girls in my year. My friends say I'm pretty and thin, but I want to hear this from him. I want to know why he won't go out with me although I'm too embarrassed to ask him myself as I'm quite shy. Maybe I'm ugly and too fat for him? I'm comfortable around him and he's easy to have fun with, but I want to be more than just friends. Can I have some advice about how to attract him? Mary.

Answer

Tell him how you feel – unless you speak up you'll never know what he wants. But please don't imagine there's anything wrong with you just because this boy isn't desperate to make a date. The fact is some boys won't want to go out with you – it's only special people with similar interests you can really get along with.

Rejection hurts

I fancy one of the boys in my class but he just doesn't want to know me. I've tried so many times to get his attention but it's always the same answer – no. I've got to the stage of asking my parents to move me to a different school. I've told some people but they just laughed saying I was silly and will get over it. What shall I do? I love him so much! Mandy.

Answer

You're not silly. Love is real. But you have to accept his No as a No. Tell yourself to give him up as a bad job. When you do, perhaps you would like to cry, or shout, or sulk? That's the way to get over someone – letting your hair down.

Flashy friend

I'm sixteen years old and in love with a girl in my year but my best buddy loves her, too! I've thought of asking her out before him but I haven't got as much flair as him. Gary.

Answer

Remind yourself that flash isn't all. Loads of people like honesty, even modesty. There are enough bigheads in the world. Just tell your mate you can't help yourself, you've got to see if she'll go out with you. Then say to her, 'I want to be your friend more than I've ever wanted anything.'

Dumping ground

I've been going out with a girl for two years but in the last couple of months I've seen her less and less. She always sounds as if something is on her mind. I think she's trying to 'dump' me but is too shy to do it. I've also found out that she fancies a boy down her street a lot. Shall I 'dump' her? Signed, Confused of Croydon.

Answer

No – ask if your suspicions are true. You don't want to lose her if this is a big misunderstanding. Maybe she's got a problem and is dying for your help? If she has 'moved on', you can call it a day and drop each other.

In love with TV star

I've been madly in love with a boy who used to act in a children's television series, but recently left. I'm very depressed since I know I'll never meet him but that doesn't stop me wishing I could go out with him. He's the only boy I really fancy. I've tried to fall for boys my own age (twelve) but it never works out. I'm beginning to think he's the only boy I'll ever love and I want to marry him. I even found out which school he goes to. Please can you give me some advice on how to stop loving him since it's not just a crush that lasts five minutes. Anna R.

Answer

You feel confused – you want to marry him *and* stop loving him! But it isn't 'just a crush'. Loving someone you can't meet feels exceptionally painful. However, I promise this won't spoil the rest of your life. On the contrary, you're more likely to have a successful romantic future because you can 'feel all your feelings'. So worry not. The confusions will pass. There will be boyfriends one day, and offers of marriage, if that's what you want, from the opposite sex. Cut this letter out and stick it on your mirror – and see if I'm right.

Disapproving mum

There's this boy at school that I really like. I've been out with him seven times before but that was at Junior School. Now we've moved to Senior School we are in separate classes. Sometimes I think he likes me and sometimes I'm not so sure. I've asked my mum what I should do and she said that if I ask him out he'll just use me and that I should wait and see if he asks me. I can't wait that long. It's driving me crazy. I'm nearly twelve. Megan.

Answer

Your mum wants what's best for you but she may not realize that these days girls do ask boys out. Tell her it's just as likely that someone will 'use' you if you wait for them to make all the running. They may expect to boss you about, even. Is that what she's after?

Age-Gap?

I am eleven years of age and I have a crush on a boy who is fourteen and goes to my future school. He said that people would call him cradle-snatcher if he went out with me. Would they really call him that? Does age really matter that much? Laura.

Answer

It doesn't matter to everybody, and it doesn't matter when you're older but that's not the point. The point is it matters to this boy. You can't force him to go out with you and maybe you won't want to when you remember how much he's fussed about his reputation?

Age-gap again

I recently went on holiday and I really fancied a boy leader. I went to all of the workshops he was doing. One night the whole group went to the beach for a barbecue and I had my photo taken with him. The next day he sat next to me at lunch. The trouble is he's eighteen and going out with my dorm leader and I'm fourteen. I find myself crying over him and thinking about him all the time. Unless I go on the same holiday next year I'll never see him again. He liked me and I have his address but I'm afraid to write to him in case he gets the wrong idea (well, the right idea!) I don't want him to know I fancy him. HELP! Anon.

Answer

Since you don't want to let on you love him yet also want some contact, I suggest you write a letter saying how much you enjoyed the holiday and look forward to seeing everyone again next year. Then you might get a personal reply and feel a little bit closer to him. The problem has no easy answer but you're entitled to your feelings.

Age-gap 3

I'm an eleven-year-old girl and I'm totally in love with a seventeen-year-old guy. He's a rough guy at school and he drinks alcohol as well as smokes. I've never spoken to him because I'm a very shy girl and when I see him I run inside and watch him through the window. I wish I could just have a conversation with the guy and maybe we will get to love each other, or maybe just go out together. I've spoken to my mum about it but she said he's too old for me. What do you think? Angela.

Answer

I agree with your mum. In a few years' time, the age gap won't matter a fig, but it is a problem now. I don't think it's fair on him either.

Age-gap 4

Please help me. I want to die. I'm in love with a 'Mr X' whose wife is friends with my mum. After telling a few people I love him, Mr X somehow found out! When his wife heard too, things went disastrously wrong. My mum grounded me for three months and told me never to fancy him again. But I do, I can't help it! I've fancied him for over two years. How can I stop it when all he does is talk to me whenever possible, making me love him more? Everyone thinks I hate him and that's what I imply. But deep down inside I love him more than anything on the planet!!!!! PS He is twenty years older than me – HELP! A Kevin Costner fan.

Answer

Dear Five Exclamation Marks, Your mum can't stop you fancying anyone, but she can certainly insist you don't see Mr X on your own or get further involved. You're going to have to be grown up about this because all the adults are going to foil you – including X himself. Sometimes you cannot have what you want, even though it's true love. There's some comfort in telling yourself 'You can control my body but not my mind, and even though I failed, Mr X missed a wonderful experience.'

Age-gap 5

Please, Phillip, can you sort out a disagreement I am having with three of my friends? The disagreement is about whether a lad of 21 should go out with a 14-16-year-old! I say that it is all right but my friends say that it is wrong. Please can you tell me who is right or wrong? Gratefully, Mark, Burnley.

Answer

You're both right and wrong because it just depends. It depends first on how grown-up the people are and second on what you mean by 'going out with'. For example, it is legal for a girl of sixteen to marry a boy of 21 (with her parents' consent). And it's fine for anyone to be 'just friends' with anyone else. But it is against the law for a 21-year-old boy to sleep with a girl who is under the age of sixteen.

Age-gap 6

I am thirteen years old and I am going out with a seven-year-old boy. He's sweet and nice and acts thirteen. He's good at singing and he gives me lots of stories and songs he's made up. I don't care if I am seven years older than him, but all my friends think I'm mad to be doing this. My mum does not know. Please help. 'Angela' (not my real name).

Answer

It's great that you share so much and there's nothing wrong with being friends provided he can cope. The only trouble is you probably won't have much in common in a year or two's time so please don't break his heart.

Age-gap 7

Please can you help me with my embarrassing problem? It's starting to get out of hand now and I'm desperately seeking help. I'm thirteen years old and I've fallen in love with an 89-year-old man who lives in the same street as me. He's a widower and is very handsome, kind and gentle even though he doesn't look 89. Nobody knows about my problem. I'd be too embarrassed if I told my parents. What should I do?

Answer

Of course you can fall in love with anyone of any age. But I do think a 76-year age gap stands in the way of your future. Be friends, by all means, but let your parents know where you are.

Needs confidence

I'm a fifteen-year-old girl and I've liked this boy in my year for over ten months. He's very kind, caring and shy. I know this may sound stupid but I think I've fallen in love with him. I think he knows I like him because I'm forever staring at him and he stares back, although we rarely speak. Every minute of the day my thoughts drift to him and he's always in my dreams. I'm totally obsessed with him. I know he doesn't have a girlfriend but he's friends with lots of girls, so I never have the guts to talk to him. Please help me as there are definitely no more fish in the sea for me. A Frustrated Lover.

Answer

There's nothing wrong in being in love. The coast is clear since you know he doesn't have a girlfriend. So the only thing holding you back is yourself. If he's worth dreaming about, he's worth approaching. But nothing will happen unless you make this move since he's just as shy as you. Smile, ask him how he's doing and would he like to come round and hear your new tapes? Imagine you are one of the confident characters from your favourite TV serial while you do it – and tell me how it goes on.

Love is in the air

There's a girl in my class. Every time I see her I want to swing her round in my arms and kiss her. I love her so much I want her to be my own. Bobby.

Answer

Then show her this letter and say it's from you. I think she'd be impressed to discover how romantic you are.

Tongue-tied

Last year, I went to a concert with my best friend and his sister (sixteen). Soon after, I asked her out but she refused, though she still wants us to be good friends. Since her brother is my best friend I get to see her all the time. But when I'm with her, I can't express my feelings. How can I say I love her and show my affection without upsetting her? Confused fifteen-year-old.

Answer

This is difficult for you but not impossible. She has said she wants to remain friendly so don't hide your feelings. As long as you don't harass her she can't object to you being nice. If you really love her you won't turn yourself off like a tap. And maybe she'll notice?

How do you know?

I have a crush on a boy and I think he likes me. But I am not sure, so I don't know whether to ask him out. I would like you to try and help me decide if he likes me. I will not ask him out unless I am certain he likes me. Puzzled Teenager.

Answer

The whole trouble is you can never be sure that a stranger really likes you. Even if they do, they might play a game and not admit it. So if you wait till you are absolutely certain before speaking you will never get your mouth open, nor ever go out. I know you are afraid of rejection. But embarrassment won't kill you, so take a chance. If he says no, you did your best. Maybe you did get it wrong but the loss is his.

Holiday romance

A few weeks ago, I went on holiday to Spain and there I fell in love with the waiter that sometimes served us. My dad told him that I liked him and a few times he kissed me for fun. This made leaving him feel so much worse. I have been home for four weeks now and I can't stop thinking about him. I keep looking at his photo and wishing I was still there with him. A few times I have had dreams about him and every time someone mentions his name I keep wanting to cry as I know I cannot see him again till next year. My mum says it is just a crush and I will get over it. But I know I am really in love with him and I don't know what to do. I know he isn't married but he is a few years older than me and I know it can't work out, but this doesn't change the way I feel. Help! LT.

Answer

Your feelings are real. Love is love is love. It can hurt at any age. So don't ignore what has happened (as if you could!). You say yourself there are practical obstacles. But that doesn't mean you can't think, pine, talk, smile, wish, hope, write, sing, shout and cry. What your mum should really do (tell her) is encourage you to enjoy this feeling of love even if it can't take you to Spain just yet. I promise it won't kill you not having him. But it will upset you to be told you're being silly, so fight back.

Long-distance romance

I have been friendly with this girl for about a year and a half and I am very keen on her and would like to go out with her. The trouble is I live in Bristol and she lives in Manchester. Is it possible to go out with somebody when they live so far away and if so what will it involve? Doug, fourteen.

Answer

It's possible. You must have overcome some of the distance to be friendly at all. But it's not convenient. First, you wouldn't be able to meet often – the journey takes hours. Second, travel is expensive – I don't know if you're rich, but you'd need to be. Third, it's difficult to stay in enough touch. You sort of lose closeness. Try it if you both want, writing and phoning.

It's all yuck!

I think there is something wrong with me. I am twelve but cannot kiss or show my affections to anyone. To me, it is disgusting and sickening. I can't understand how anyone can enjoy it. I have been going out with boys and given them a peck on the cheek but I can't bring myself to kiss them. I don't think I have ever fallen in love with anyone, and that's my secret. Is it because I have never been loved by a boy so can't imagine what it is like? I don't even want to know how love feels. Lesley.

Answer

Lesley, I'd be worried if you said no one in your family loved you. Or if you said you could never show any affection to your parents or friends or even the family dog. But I don't think there's anything wrong with you just because you can't kiss boys at twelve. You are just saying you aren't ready yet, and nor is your body. (I couldn't believe the facts of life when I first heard them either – yuck!) We all develop feelings at different rates and I promise you'll realize when you are ready to love a boyfriend.

Getting his attention

Please help me. I really LOVE this boy, but every time I go to talk or something he walks away and says he'll talk to me later but he never does. Do you think that he loves me at all? If not, what should I do to get him to love me? Cassandra.

Answer

I think he's rude, or shy, or both. But I can't know whether he loves you or not. Only he can say. You need to know where you stand and take control. So next time he tries to walk off, say, 'Wait a minute. Would you really like to be friends and talk, or am I bothering you? Tell me so I can know what to do?' He will like you if he feels comfortable with you and putting him more at ease could help.

Breaking the ice

I am eleven and have just started secondary school with all my friends. There are loads from our old class and there's this boy that I really fancy. Everyone gets on with him. I have tried to be partners with him in some subjects so I can ask him out but I'm embarrassed about it. I don't know what to say or how to go about it.

Everyone gets on with him because he's funny and always cheers you up if you're glum. Please tell me what to do, I'm desperate. Jo.

Answer

This is the Number One problem in my PROBS postbag so don't think you're alone. And naturally you feel embarrassed when trying to approach a boy for the first time. You get hot and bothered because you feel anxious. 'I'm too excited to think straight. My heart's pounding. I'm afraid he will reject me and that others will laugh.' OK: work out what you want to say – 'Can we walk home together today? I really like being with you.' Tell him this when he has enough time to answer and no one will overhear. Be ready for him to say No or Yes, so you can prepare your own reactions. If it's a No, say, 'Is that a permanent No, or just No for now?' When you've made this approach, say how nervous you felt about doing it. It will help calm you. Remember to keep breathing slowly and regularly throughout so you don't dry up. And have a nice time.

What's going wrong?

My problem is girls – they won't go out with me. I try to talk to them and do everything that pleases them but they just ignore me. I wear after-shave and stuff like that. It is embarrassing because all the other boys in my class are going out with girls. What can I do? Alan.

Answer

This is the second biggest problem in my PROBS postbag! The tough answer is that girls don't go out with bottles of after-shave. They go out with people. Smelling nice helps, but that won't do the trick by itself.

You need to concentrate on natural behaviour rather than a plot. In order to get a girlfriend, you have got to be genuinely interested in her. That means talking about her life, feelings, hopes, wishes and fears. That means listening well, reacting and smiling. You actually have to concentrate! It's an advantage if you can be funny, but don't worry if you can't. Practise having better conversations with your family and friends to begin with.

Silly boy

I have a problem. No one likes my boyfriend and now he is starting to act silly. My best friend said I should get rid of him. If I do I will be upset because I still like him but he is always silly. What shall I do? Melanie – aged ten.

Answer

It's very important to accept people as they are. So you must accept that your boyfriend is sometimes a bit daft *and* that your friends don't think he's wonderful. That's OK. It would be a very silly world where everyone liked everyone, and he's your boyfriend, not theirs.

Grief

I have a problem. The closest boy I have ever met has died and several times I have nearly killed myself but I know I wouldn't. I don't think I can survive without him. Please help. Mary, aged eleven.

Answer

I don't believe you are going to kill yourself either. I think your letter means: 'This was the nicest boy I ever knew. When he died, my heart broke. It felt like I would never enjoy myself again. I get sad all through. It's like the bit of me that can fall in love has been killed. I don't know how to bear these feelings.' Grief does this to you. You will survive. But just for a while, you will feel as if your life has also stopped. Please tell someone how much it is hurting.

Bad behaviour

I have a problem. I fancy a boy called M— and he has just asked me out. I said yes. But last week he invited me to his house. When I got there, he pushed me on to his bed and started getting fresh. I pushed him off and walked out. I see him every day at school and every time I look at him he says 'Just you wait'. I don't know what to do. Please help. Fiona, Glasgow.

Answer

You clearly like M, but not his behaviour which is rude and crude. You need to educate him as well as yourself. Instead of putting up with these threatening, smouldering looks, go and talk to him. Say you did not like being jumped on the other day and it upset you. Tell him what a bad move it was if he wants to get a girl. Then see if he'd like to come round to your house (when you know someone else will be on the premises). If he's really worth pursuing, he'll be able to cope. If not, forget it.

Love from afar

I am in love with a girl who is in a year above me and I hardly know her. I think she likes me. I'm eleven. Please give me some advice. Stuart, Plymouth.

Answer

Then get to know her. It's jolly difficult walking up to a stranger and saying 'I love you'. By comparison, it would be easy to nod, smile, offer her a bit of your chocolate and ask her what she thought about last night's telly (or pop videos, or clothes or horoscopes etc). She may not respond but you won't get anywhere by worshipping from afar, will you? Then if you click, you can become more personal (but not during the first chat – give it a while).

Breaking the rules

I have a crush on my teacher. A few weeks ago I told him and he started kissing me. He asked if I would like to go out for a meal. What should I say? Yes or no? Katie, aged thirteen.

Answer

No, because all the rules say he shouldn't be touching you. You could break your heart. He could lose his job – or end up in court if things go further. No, because tho' it's good to feel loving it's bad to have guilty secrets. They only screw up your feelings. I think you would be reluctant to tell your parents you were dating this man, wouldn't you? Yet crushes are not silly and the feelings are genuinely strong. They show you are learning how to love. The important thing is to enjoy them without getting hurt. That means not staking your life on them. But strangely they always feel worse if you are insecure or unhappy at home. So ask yourself whether you are not covering up some other pain in the process? Find a good friend to talk to, an aunt, a woman teacher, a school counsellor, someone who won't blab, then let it all out.

Dealing with rejection

I hope you can help me with my problem. I am fourteen and have been going out with a boy called Darren (who is eleven – I know it's silly). We were getting on really well till he didn't meet me one night at the disco. Now he says he's finished with me and going out with someone else. I am so confused and sad and depressed. Belinda.

Answer

Please don't say it's silly. If you care about someone and they dump you it always hurts. Whether you are nine or 90, rejection takes away your confidence. You are telling yourself nobody else will want you. OK – say that. Let out the sadness. Soon you will find yourself feeling calmer. What Darren does is up to him. Maybe he is wonderful. Maybe he's a twerp. But if you share this unhappy feeling with those around you, I promise it will change and you will realize Darren is not your judge and jury.

All-girls' school

I am twelve years old and I go to a girls' school. I'm afraid that I won't have a boyfriend by the time I am fifteen. Please help me as I really want a boyfriend.

Answer

I bet half the girls in your school aged fifteen have got boyfriends and the other half aren't talking. I know it feels more difficult at a single-sex school but there are the holidays to look forward to – not to mention school dances, plays etc. – when boys turn up. It will happen.

In love with teacher

I need your help. The problem is I'm having an affair with my English teacher. After the lesson we have a ten-minute break so we can kiss and stuff. We've done a lot more than that after school hours. We always use condoms. I know it's not a good thing to do but when I'm with him I feel differently. I don't care what people might say if they knew. Anyway, I've told you this because he's afraid that the head-teacher is on the verge of finding out, so he's going to work many miles away. He has asked me to go with him. I am aware we are breaking the law but I really don't care because this relationship means so much to me. I need your help. Thank you. From a desperate fifteen-year-old.

Answer

He's breaking the law and could be sent to prison for his offence. You are said to be the 'victim'. But legal questions aside, are you ready to cope with the big possibility that you'll be dumped if things get too hot? Is his offer to support you serious? Are your parents going to stand by and let all this happen? You need to stop thinking with your hormones and work the practicalities out on paper. There's nothing wrong with love. When you're sixteen there's no legal objection to sex. What's wrong is pretending there are no other problems. Get real – and whatever you do, don't get pregnant.

Lonely girl

This problem may sound stupid, but I can't help the way I feel. I have a great family and lots of friends, but I still want a boyfriend. At night I pretend that my make-believe boyfriend is in bed with me and that we are making love. Then I touch myself all over and pretend it's my boyfriend. Phillip, you've just got to help me. Why do I feel like this? Is it normal? I need your help as I feel embarrassed to talk to anyone else. Anon, twelve years old.

Answer

This couldn't be more normal – as your hormones rise during puberty, so your fantasies focus on sex and love. When you haven't got a boyfriend, your mind sort of invents one. Please don't worry.

Fancies the boss

I work in a newsagent's and I fancy the manageress. I am fourteen and she is about 26. What do I do? Do I show her that I love her somehow? Or do I just leave it? Please help. A confused fourteen-year-old.

Answer

Just do your paper round and enjoy this as a fantasy.

In love with older man

I'm a fourteen-year-old girl and in desperate need of help. About two years ago I started to fancy older men in their twenties and never took any notice of boys my own age. As I look about five years older than I am, these men fancied me too. Then one day I met this really nice man who is 26. We got on together very well. After two months we were madly in love. One night when I was at his flat (my parents thought I was at a friend's) one thing led to another and we ended up making love on the floor. Now when we are apart I miss him making love to me and touching me. I always look forward to our nights together, but now he says I must tell my parents about us and I'm worried about what they will do as I don't want to stop seeing him. Please help. Anon.

Answer

He's trying to tell you his feelings have changed. I guess he's scared of the consequences of having illegal sex with you – maybe he's also moved on in his feelings. I wonder if he still loves you? If he does, will he wait until you two can be together legally? Otherwise, I should cut your losses now.

Best friend's boyfriend

I'm writing to you because my best friend has a boyfriend but he also fancies me. He asked me out and I said yes. We went to a disco and he asked me back to his house. We got a bit carried away and nearly had sex. I'm fifteen years old and I don't know what to tell my best friend. I don't want to lose her but I really fancy him and I don't regret any of it. Alex.

Answer

If you carry on, she's going to find out anyway. I suggest you ask the young man to choose between the two of you. Then explain things to your friend if you need to.

Confused by boy

I've fancied this guy for ages, then he asked me out. I guessed it was for a joke – and it was! The thing is, he

keeps playing this joke when he sees me. He either asks
me out or says something to show his 'love'. There have
been a few times when we were supposed to meet, but
he never came. Everybody knows now and it is really
embarrassing. I try to ignore and forget him, but when I
see him I do just the opposite! My work is suffering and
I don't eat much as a result. I still fancy him! Please
help. Joan.

Answer

Oh come on, he's just a pest. If you do find yourself
weakening, play him at his own game – 'OK – but I'll
only go out with you for a joke!'

Getting serious

I am only ten years old and I have a boyfriend. We love
each other very much and hate to be apart. We have
been on a few dates and it's getting quite serious. I can't
stop wondering what it would be like to have sex with
him. We frenchie a lot. My mum's friends might see me
on my dates with him and then I would be in serious
trouble. Please help! Beth.

Answer

Then you'd better calm down. The best idea is to ask
your mum if he can see you at your house 'just as a
friend'. That way she can gradually get used to the
whole idea.

Boyfriend going too far

I'm eight years old and I went to my boyfriend's house
to sleep. When we were upstairs he started to undress me and try and kiss me all over. I really like him

but he's going too far. He is ten. Jane.

Answer

He certainly is. Tell him to keep his hands to himself or you'll tell on him.

Needs courage 1

I fancy this boy who is in the same year as me at school. I sent him a letter telling him how I felt and asking him to go out with me. He said no. Some of my close friends said that he will probably say yes if I go up to him and ask him in the flesh, but I don't know if I can pluck up the courage to do it. What should I do? Alice.

Answer

You've nothing to lose and all to gain by speaking up. Even if your friends are setting you up, it might work!

Needs courage 2

I've fallen in love with the most gorgeous boy ever. I think he likes me because he's always putting his arm round me and stares at me in lessons. I haven't the courage to ask him out. My best friend asked him out for me. He said I had to ask him myself, but I daren't. Please could you suggest a way of me going out with him without me having to ask him out. A madly-in-love-girl, aged thirteen.

Answer

No. See the answer above (though I do understand what you're feeling).

Needs courage 3

I am thirteen years old. I really like a girl in my class but every time I try to ask her out I just go all shy and make a fool of myself and she thinks I'm just babyish. What shall I do? Kieron.

Answer

You could be less tough on yourself for a start. It is hard at any age to find the courage to ask someone for a date. Rejection is always a possibility and nobody welcomes that. It's even harder when you are doing it for perhaps the first time. So try praising yourself for getting this far. Second, I'm sure you're wrong about her feeling you're babyish. That's *your* feeling which you are dumping on her. You see, it hasn't crossed your mind that she might *like* to be asked out. And she probably would. And she probably feels nervous too! So work out what you want to say to her. Practise the words a bit at home. Make sure the right film is playing at the cinema. Choose a time when she's not surrounded by friends or dashing off. Remember to smile. Speak clearly. And who knows. You'll be writing to me next about being too young to go steady.

Doesn't like him back

A boy at school likes me and he's getting on my nerves. I don't like him. He makes me sick. I'm an eleven-year-old girl and very depressed. He always chases me home after school. Please can you help me? Debbie.

Answer

Ask your mum to pick you up from school one day and tell him to stop bothering you.

Likes ugly girl

I've recently started at a new school and I've found a girl I like. This girl wears glasses, has ginger hair and is not attractive. I'm afraid that if I ask her out all the other boys will laugh at me because she's ugly. What should I do? Mark.

Answer

Beauty is subjective and glasses are wonderful. Why let other people make your own decisions for you? When friends tease, say 'You don't know what you're talking about' and walk away.

Rotten ex-boyfriend

I was going out with a boy that I fancied for ages. The other day he dumped me. I was really cut up about it and I cried because I was so upset. The very next day he asked my best friend out and she said yes. Now he's always kissing her and putting his arm round her when he knows I'm looking just to get at me. I can't stand him any more, but should I break up with my best friend because of this? I'm beginning to hate her, too. Please help. Confused Gloria.

Answer

It's only natural to resent your friend for making such a quick move on your boyfriend. But how much more satisfying to stay friends with her whatever he does.

Why should he steal her from you too? Treat him like a puppy who's being a nuisance. Boys come and go but you need your best friend.

Wants more than just friends

There's a girl I have always fancied ever since I came to the school a year ago. I plucked up courage and asked her out but she said no. This has been happening up until now. Then last week I went to a disco party and she was there. I danced with her and gave her a kiss and she didn't pull away from me. I then asked her out and she said she'd think about it. I came back to school and she then said ... *no*! – just friends. I'm afraid I don't really want to be friends but to go out with her. What shall I do? From Harry, aged twelve.

Answer

Harry, you've had your answer and I'm afraid you must live with it. I think there's more chance of her changing her mind if you stop pushing and settle for becoming friends.

In love and jealous

I'm eleven and I think I'm in love already. I can't sleep at night and I want to be near him all the time. The other day we were playing dares and he got dared to snog this other girl. After they had finished I got up and thumped her. Am I in love? Wendy.

Answer

Your violence indicates more jealousy than love but I think it's fair to say you've got strong, possessive feelings. You don't need to thump your rivals – just tell your boyfriend he risks losing you.

Lost love

I'm a twelve-year-old boy who's just lost a friend (girl). It was on a campout. We had come from different towns. She asked me out about three days before the end of the camp. I just ignored her as we only had three days left. It came to the last day and we hugged each other and said goodbye. She said she was not going to come next year. I just turned away seeming not to mind, but I was crying inside. I was going to say 'I love you' but I lost the nerve and got on my bus. I wish I had got her address. I now start crying every time I think about her. Can you help? From David.

Answer

Yes, write her a letter putting down all the feelings you kept to yourself. Send it to the people who organized the camp and ask them to forward it. Even if you two never meet again (and let's hope for the best), this will ease your sadness and you can start living.

Phillip Fan

I have a problem. I'm very much in love with you. I love your face and eyes. I want a naked photo of you. I dream about you all the time. The problem is that I haven't got any pals left. They call me nuts and I don't know why. Could you please print your address so I can come and we can do things together? From Antonia, seventeen.

Answer

No, but I can see that you really need to go out and

make some new friends. You're having these fantasies because there's no one else to play with. Join a sports club, go hill-walking, do aerobics, start drama classes, learn to use a computer, give a party – anything to meet people. And since I'm spoken for, it's time to get very close to someone else, isn't it?

Are fantasies OK?

For about two years now, I have been infatuated with an actor. Every time I see a photograph of him, or watch one of his films, my stomach turns upside-down because he's so handsome. It is against my religion to fall in love with someone or go out with a boy, unless you are married. I cannot tell my best friend because she would disapprove and I don't want to damage our relationship. What can an infatuated twelve-year-old do? Malti.

Answer

You can understand that what may be against your religion is not against your imagination. Fantasies are not reality. You won't be breaking any rules just by thinking loving thoughts. This dramatic passion is a type of rehearsal, preparing you to fall in love for real when the time (and rules) may be right.

She's tried everything

I am in my teens and desperate for your advice. I know you won't print this letter as it sounds silly but I am heartbroken. I am in love with a boy called Craig. I know he takes the mickey out of me because I'm very overweight. I'm nearly 13 stone but I'm quite tall which compensates a bit. Also he has a very pretty girlfriend he would never finish with. I have even tried to bribe him with money to go out with me. I've tried spreading rumours about her but that only got people to hate me. I told them she was pregnant but it isn't true. I have no friends and cannot talk to my parents as I'm too embarrassed. Chris.

Answer

Falling in love with Craig is not the real problem. You've obviously never managed to fall in love with yourself. Without some self-love it's very hard to make friends or run a romance. I don't blame you for feeling rotten, or for trying to buy Craig's affection, or for comfort-eating. But you have to rescue your self-confidence. Have a look at Anne Dickson's book *A Woman In Your Own Right* (Quartet Books).

Football-mad guy

I'm eleven years old and I've only had one boyfriend but he wasn't right for me. I wanted him to be with me all the time but all he was interested in was football. He never kissed me. He didn't even try. He was good-looking but boring. Then I caught him hugging another girl. I asked for an explanation but his excuse was poor. So I chucked him. I really regret chucking him because now I don't have a boyfriend. Melissa.

Answer

You will. But remember that hunky looks aren't everything. There's no point in being a soccer widow at eleven. So go for a guy with more gift of the gab.

Crushed by keep-fit instructor

I am a fourteen-year-old girl and I am madly in love with my mum's 23-year-old fitness instructor. He comes to our house every Sunday to train my mum, and sometimes I join in. He's so hunky and gorgeous and kind, and he is so funny – he's always making me laugh. My mum who is 37 and my dad, 43, know I fancy him and just laugh. They say it's just a crush but it isn't. I told 'Victor' how I felt about him, and he just smiled, and said I was too young. Last week I kissed him suddenly before he could stop me. The problem is he told my mum he can't come on Sundays any more, but he can on Wednesdays when I'm at school. He's avoiding me, I know it. I'm so upset and I'm always crying. What can I do? Doreen.

Answer

Heartbreak is heartbreak at any age. What you feel is more difficult because Victor is your first. But he has a say in this too. I know it's tough, but what Victor says is *no*. It doesn't matter what his reasons are, whether concern for you or fear of the law. Love is about respecting other people's choices. You must respect his. It's hard for parents to see how fast their children grow up but at least tell mum you're sad even if you can't say why.

Just William

I'm in love with a student maths teacher called William. I'll be very upset when he leaves the school in June. He knows I love him. When I get him for maths, I can't help staring at him. My mum said I should tell him how I feel but I haven't got the guts. I think I should try to hate him but I find it impossible. What do you think? When I stare at him I feel like I am locked on to his eyes – they are really nice. I am fourteen and three-quarters. Ellen.

Answer

I think you should respect your feelings. Of course you're going to miss him and the best way to cope is to tell him, 'I've liked you more than any other teacher I've had' and give him a nice going-away present. Discuss it further with mum and you'll be OK.

Caught in the act

I'm fifteen, and I was quite serious about my sixteen-year-old boyfriend until the other night. He turned up to meet me with a great big lovebite on his neck. He says he did it at work where his gold chain pinched his skin. I want to believe him and get back with him but my parents say he's cheating on me and I'm being pathetic. Hesta.

Answer

It would take a chain of gold bars to make a mark like a lovebite! You have to decide whether he's worth keeping on despite the fact that he clearly snogged someone else, then made a pathetic excuse afterwards. Don't be misled – if you get back together tell him he's on probation.

In love with GP

I'm in love with my GP, a beautiful woman in her thirties. The trouble is I'm only fifteen. I've known her for two months although I haven't said anything yet.

She would be my ideal partner. She has brains and a perfect, model-girl figure. I'd like to ask her for a date but I'm a bit bothered about her husband. Also she might turn me down. Andrew.

Answer

She might indeed. The husband might prescribe something stronger. I'm afraid this is a dream. There's nothing wrong in having crushes but you can't act on them. Look for a girl in your own age-group who has the same qualities, brains and style.

Vulnerable

I'm a thirteen-year-old girl who has just lost her mother in a car crash. The driver was drunk at the time. This hurt me very much. In school there's this really nice boy. He asked me out and I don't know what to say as I'm afraid if anything happened to him I would get hurt just like when my mum died. Please help me. Vera.

Answer

You're right to be careful. For you especially, it's natural to worry about the risks of losing someone if you get too close. However, you sound ready to start a relationship and this boy might be just what the doctor ordered. He might make you feel life is good again – so don't dwell on the thought of disaster.

Wheelchair friend

I'm going out with a boy who's in a wheelchair. I really fancy him but everybody in my class at school makes fun of me because of his wheelchair. I try to ignore them but it's really getting at me. Why is this and why do they do it? Maureen.

Answer

Because they are frightened by his 'weakness'. Because he's easy to pick on. And because you don't like it. Bullies are the true weaklings so don't let them get you down. You're worth ten times any of them.

Ignored by old flame

When I was eleven I fell for this boy of fifteen. Near where I live there's a mass of woods. He took me up there. We started to kiss and we couldn't stop. Now I'm twelve, I've moved into the same school as him and he just ignores me. I don't know whether I've done something wrong or not. When I think about him I get all depressed. Nina.

Answer

I'm not surprised – he seems to have left you in the lurch. His action was neither kind nor grown-up. In fact, he's shown himself to be really immature, so maybe it's best to move on.

Pushing him around

I'm a fourteen-year-old girl. I fancy a lad in my science group but he doesn't fancy me. I try to get him to notice me by touching him in places I shouldn't. I want to kiss him. My friends say that I'm stupid but I just can't seem to stop myself. I get all hot and bothered when he talks to me. Also when I'm in bed I fantasize that he's in there with me. Please help. Patsy.

Answer

Hormones are hell. You feel very physical about this boy but your direct approach has simply scared him off. An old-fashioned 'Hello' would break the ice better than an unwanted prod. You could then hope to start a proper conversation (kisses come later).

Glimpse of bra

I think I'm in love with this girl because a few months ago I saw her bra through her shirt. This girl is the same age as me. I've never had a proper girlfriend before. I just can't find the guts to ask her out because every time I see her I get excited. Malcolm.

Answer

Love is longing for one person. That's not the same as glimpsing a girl's underwear. What you feel then is 'desire'! This is normal. Tell yourself you haven't lost your heart and it will be OK to ask her out.

Broken-hearted

I'm a fourteen-year-old female who recently met a lovely fifteen-year-old boy. We started having a great relationship. We did foreplay but never had sexual intercourse. This went on for more than three wonderful weeks. I felt as if I really loved him and he said he loved me but the last time I spoke to him he told me it wasn't worth us continuing. I can't believe it. I keep wondering if it's because we didn't have sexual intercourse or if he has just gone off me? I feel so empty and depressed and have even considered taking my life. Trish.

Answer

Please don't think of dying for this feeble fella. The relationship made you feel great but he must have been putting it on. You were dead right not to sleep with him because he didn't value *you*. Try to nurse your broken heart while looking for someone sincere.

Two boys to fancy

I'm going out with this boy whom I love very much, and who is very rich and intelligent. The problem is another boy fancies me as well. They're both very handsome and I'm attracted to both of them. I don't know whether to keep going out with my recent boyfriend or go out with this other boy. We're all fourteen. Christine.

Answer

I think one of the problems here is that you think you should behave like a much older woman – say, someone of 25 or 30 – who ought to know her own mind and be going steady. But how on earth can you decide what you want from blokes before you've had enough experience to work out your preferences? Practical experiment is the only way in which you can discover how you feel about boys, their wealth, good looks and intelligence in relation to your own needs. Frankly, your 'job' as a teenager is to keep your options open and learn as you go along. There's plenty of time later on to specialize in a super fella and by then you will know how to do it! So the broad answer to your question is about your attitude. Don't feel tied down. Don't feel guilty about playing the field. Don't worry about having four or five boyfriends or male friends and don't think life has to be too restrained – this is the time to have fun. Make it plain to boys you know that you belong to yourself. They should be told that you go on dates with other people. Be open about it. No one is ready to 'settle down' at fourteen. Don't close any doors – going out with 'Mark' on Monday doesn't mean you won't see 'Bill' again the following week. Try to work out what really matters to you – rich boyfriends, or caring boyfriends. Of course, if you can find a rich *and* caring fella, that might seem quite a bonus. Notice how you feel inside – if your heart pulls you towards someone very special then start listening.

Holiday romance

I'm a thirteen-year-old girl and last summer met a sixteen-year-old boy on holiday. We spent every evening together until he went home. I've written to him several times but haven't yet had a reply. I think about him every night but I won't tell anyone because I just think they will make fun of me. He was my first boyfriend so I don't know how to handle this. Please advise me. Paula.

Answer

You two got very close very quickly and lots of strong new feelings started up which can easily make you feel embarrassed. That's why you may not want to talk about them. Naturally, you also miss the intimacy. It's bewildering to focus on someone so completely then have to separate when the holiday ends. The sensation is almost one of bereavement, as if someone has died. I also bet you're furious he hasn't bothered to answer your letters. Perhaps he's not very good at putting thoughts into words or is unused to correspondence but his action seems rude and rejecting. The least he could do was say your letters got there! The way to recover is not to stay silent but to share your sadness, as you have with me. Take consolation from knowing that you are the one maturing and growing and this will bring you success with boys in the future. Don't despair. Even though it hurts now you can be proud of learning to love like an adult. Write again and tell him he's a clod for not replying. Even if he never answers at least you're giving yourself the vital message 'I matter!'. Try to confide in someone you trust – if not mum, then perhaps an aunt or teacher. You don't have to give all the details just say, 'I'm a bit sad about missing someone I met.' When you feel really low, keep telling yourself 'He's the bigger loser – I'm going to love again.'

Jealousy

My girlfriend and I are both sixteen years old. We have been going out with each other for nearly a year now. The problem is that if she just glances at another boy I get jealous. I cannot help this. I daren't send for any leaflets through the post because if they were intercepted by my mother or father we would all die of embarrassment. I am very ashamed of this feeling. Will.

Answer

First of all tell yourself that some degree of jealousy is normal. If your girlfriend started to deceive you it would be natural to explode. This isn't 'primitive' but how we are. Second, accept that your family tends to be easily embarrassed. I'd hate to think your parents would actually open your letters. But it's a big handicap if they suffer from instant blushing at every misunder-standing. This doesn't help you become comfortable with your feelings. Third, extreme (or pathological) jealousy is usually about someone's inner anxieties, not what the other person has done to them. You will have to look inside yourself to find the cause and cure. When next you feel jealous about your girlfriend, sit down and talk. Get her to say things like 'What are you really feeling?' – 'Have you ever felt like this before?' This will almost certainly make you remember a time or times when you felt bitterly rejected. Talk it through, as often as you need. What do you now think of the people today? As you get more comfortable with yourself, practise being 'less jealous' by chatting about other attractive people you both see in the street. Finally, remember that she wants to be with you. The closer she feels, the more she'll want to stay. Jealous behaviour, on the other hand, has the opposite effect.

On and off

I really fancy this boy – the next day I can't bear the idea of him touching me. I desperately want a boyfriend but how will I keep one if I feel like this? My friends don't have this trouble. Maya.

Answer

One of the perils of puberty is bad timing. This works in several ways. For instance, of three girls aged thirteen one may be slim-hipped, short and flat-chested; the second may be approaching adult height, showing breast-buds and her first pubic hair; the third may be a tall, rounded, fully-developed, confident female. How can they all be expected to lead similar lives? The second area of bad timing concerns these 'in-between' feelings. You are no longer a child, so some days you want an adult lifestyle. But you are not yet fully grown-up, so on other days you only want to be looked after. On Monday, you are desperate for a proper love affair. On Tuesday, you want to sit at home, eat cereal and watch children's TV. Emotionally, you are not quite ready for regular dating. Don't worry. This stage doesn't last for ever. Before long, you'll meet someone with whom a friendship will just take off. Often when you feel out of your depth with people it is because they are trying to take things too fast for you anyway. So respect your instincts. Only allow serious petting when two conditions are right – when you yearn for it but also feel comfortable with its intensity.

Making friends

I'm fourteen and believe nobody likes me. I've actually been all the way with a boy now and he still doesn't like me. Chloe.

Answer

So now you've learned that even having sex with boys is not enough to buy you friendship. Obviously, it is horrible to think nobody likes you. But try to compare notes with girlfriends. Work out how your family behaves differently from theirs. See how you've actually been given a pretty low opinion of yourself by some of those closest to you. It's probably because you haven't been surrounded by friendly people at home, perhaps having to 'bargain' for their attention, that you've come unstuck in the world outside. You don't quite know how to make the 'boundaries' of friendship work. Certainly, I suggest you don't sleep with a boy unless you first know two things about him. 1. His family story, way of life and reasons for liking you. 2. His understanding of your emotional needs.

2

Boys' Bodies

For boys, sexual development may start as early as 11 or as late as 16 but growth rates vary a lot. Differences in height and shape can become a source of enormous anxiety at a time when everyone wants to be 'normal' and no one wants to be the 'odd one out'. Ideas of masculinity are also strongly linked to body size and appearance – a boy in his mid-teens needs a great deal of reassurance that he WILL become a man despite the tiny chest, squeaky voice and smooth chin. It's also embarrassing to go through a time of strong physical change when your body seems to develop a sexual will all of its own.

Erections everywhere

I'm twelve years old and highly developed. My problem is erections – I average five a day. I don't get them through being excited, they just come from nowhere.

It's very embarrassing. They also happen during showers at school when I dry myself. My mind is clear when I get them. I'm not thinking of girls or anything. I need help to get over this problem and to be told what's wrong with me as it's getting me down. Ben.

Answer

There's nothing wrong with you at all. The strength of all the new sex hormones makes your body ultra-sensitive to touch. It's a bit embarrassing but these 'over-reactions' eventually calm down.

More erections

I'm fourteen and every morning I wake with a painful erection. I'm worried because at half-term I'm going with the school to France and am sleeping in a dormitory with other boys. I can't bring myself to question my parents and I don't like my family doctor. Please help. Mark.

Answer

The same thing happens to every male during the 'dream phase' of sleep. You won't be the only one and it doesn't mean you're sex mad. Just wait a few moments before getting up and the problem should subside. Going to the toilet is a big help so pack a large dressing-gown to cover up on the way.

Water babies

When I swim in my games lesson there is always a girl there that I really like. Boys are not allowed to wear shorts in the baths, we have to wear briefs. When I see this girl in her costume I get an erection and it must be obvious. Once I got excited in the water and think I climaxed. I've got to do swimming for the rest of this term. I'm worried. Can any of the girls become pregnant? John.

Answer

No, the chlorine in the pool takes care of everything. As for your embarrassment, it might help to wear a pair of black pants inside dark trunks as an extra cover-up.

Penis size 1

All the other boys have bigger penises than mine and some of them even say they have sex. I'm worried because mine doesn't seem to have changed (groan). I am nearly fourteen. David.

Answer

Since the average (unaroused) human vagina is only four inches long, how far do you want your penis to exceed this capacity? If you complain I'm missing the point (and I agree that sex is not just about intercourse), tell me what you want the extra inches for? Impressing your friends? Frightening girls? Seriously, stop telling yourself you are a cock. From what you've said, it seems you've entered puberty later than your schoolfriends. This feels basically miserable but it isn't a physical mistake. Within the next year to eighteen months, your development will occur, and first to grow will be the item in question. Some of your friends seem disproportionately big only because they have adult-sized penises on boy-sized bodies.

Penis size 2

I'm fourteen years old and desperately worried about my manhood. About a year ago I was so worried I went to see a doctor. He just said that some people have big ones and some people have little ones. My dad assured me that it would grow soon, and said that I'd wake up one morning with an adult-sized one. In the showers at school I couldn't help noticing the difference in size between my penis and my friend's. He even had fully grown pubic hairs and he's five months younger than me. Do I need to worry about this problem? Will it grow before I'm an adult? Please help. Christopher.

Answer

Well, it won't develop overnight but the crucial age is about fifteen – next year for you – by which time 'most boys' have achieved adult 'growth'. However, you need to bear in mind that puberty goes at different rates for different boys – you can start maturing as early as eight or as late as sixteen. So, for instance, it would be biologically normal for a classmate to have a deep bass voice while you're still speaking in a high treble. Three other points to remember. First, the great majority of adult penises are very much the same size when erect, between six and seven inches long. Second, many young men think they look small because they only get the foreshortened view from above but when they look at other chaps in the changing room they get the 'wide-screen shot' from the side. Thirdly, science has shown that size bears no relationship to potency – you are 'manly' whatever the geometry. Men come in every shape, size, colour and speed. Your real manhood can be found in the largest sexual organ of all – your brain.

Spot of anxiety 1

I'm a depressed, frustrated and suicidal fifteen-year-old boy. You see, my problem is embarrassing and I can't talk to anyone about it. I live with my mum and dad and neither of them would understand. The problem is that I have spots on the underside of my penis. I've tried squeezing them but it's as if they have dried and gone hard under the skin. They won't come out. It's really making my life hell. I'm too frightened to get a girlfriend and it's ruining my confidence. I've had them quite a long time (about three years) and thought they would go but they haven't. Please help me because I don't know what to do. I'm too embarrassed to go to the doctor's. Sean.

Answer

Please take comfort from the fact that I get about twenty letters every week from boys with your problem. So *almost certainly* these aren't spots at all but the large 'sebaceous' glands that develop during puberty. They have a simple job – to oil the pubic hair so it doesn't get into a tangle and pull! Boys notice them far more than girls – I've never had a letter from a girl about them. And my guess is that you're in the pink of health – though to be absolutely sure you'd have to visit the doc or go to a special clinic.

Spot of anxiety 2

I have a number of tiny projections around the base of my genitals. The doctor has told me they are merely 'sebaceous' glands and nothing to be concerned about but I'm still worried. I've been unable to find any mention of such glands in books. I'm afraid any girl I start a relationship with will be put off. If *I* didn't know that these things were sebaceous glands, how is a girl to know? I'm apparently perfectly healthy but she might think otherwise. Pierce.

Answer

Girls have sebaceous glands too. The word is also in the dictionary. These tiny vessels are there to oil your body hair so it stays healthy and doesn't get into a tangle. So if you're *still* worried, mark this page in the book.

Hairiness

I'm seventeen and haven't started shaving yet. I have no hair on my chest either. Should I see my doctor? Mike.

Answer

Your doctor would always be happy to see you when you're worried. But hairiness is a genetic lottery, depending on race, family and luck. If both parents are hairy, or 'hirsute', you are likely to be hairy too, but it's not inevitable. Further, even if your father has hair on his back, he may not have needed to begin shaving his chin until he was twenty. Individual development during puberty is extremely varied. Chest hair too may first begin to show at about the age of twelve, but not finish spreading until the early twenties, or even later. Hair on the ears, on moles, on the back of the neck, eyebrows and nostrils continues to get more widespread and wiry in the middle years (darn it).

Weighty problem

I'm a sixteen-year-old boy and everyone makes fun of me. But I want a girlfriend. Do fat boys ever get girls? Ahmed.

Answer

Yes, all the time, though fat men will probably find it easier than fat boys. Down the ages and even today, fat has been associated in the minds of some women with power and success. Then again there are those who prefer a man who won't deny himself a second piece of strawberry cheesecake on the grounds that perhaps he won't deny them the same, or similar sensuous indulgences. It's obviously in your medical interest not to be overweight. However, there is a good chance that if you eat moderately in your mid-to-late teens, much of the childhood fat will disappear. But one word of warning. If you become lithe and trim, you will probably want to pay the world back for its earlier unkindnesses. Breaking women's hearts may seem like sweet revenge. But beware of the inner damage the teasing will have caused you. One day you'll need to deal with this directly and talking about it now might prove safer than wrecking lives. PS: don't crash-diet. Don't fad-diet. They never work in the long run.

Prostitution

I foolishly rang one of those numbers you see advertised in London phone booths and had a topless massage plus hand relief from a prostitute. I have never had a girlfriend. I am now desperately worried I could have caught Aids though my brain tells me this is unlikely. I cannot get this fear out of my head. Roy.

Answer

It's most unlikely you will acquire HIV from a sex 'massage'. What you have picked up instead is an enormous dose of guilt. You feel your behaviour was wrong. Inside, you believe you ought to be punished. Yet it would be more helpful to try to understand yourself. There are some obvious thoughts to consider. Were you just curious? Did it happen because you are shy about making contact with women? Does this mean you need to improve your social skills? Do you underestimate your ordinary need for physical close-ness anyway? If it throws any light, consider the attitudes of your own family towards sex. Did they encourage or inhibit you? Best of all, try to forgive yourself for the sin of curiosity – now you know how a hooker makes money out of men.

Drunken folly

I took home this girl who said I could have sex with her. Then she passed out dead drunk. I don't much like her but I was very devastated when I couldn't make love to her even though she was completely at my mercy. Why? Josh, aged eighteen.

Answer

Why was she silly enough to give permission? Why couldn't you do it? Or why did you even try? Whatever your question, the answer must cope with your macho assumptions. First, did you really have to copulate just because the opportunity was there? Second, do you really feel compelled to go to bed with a girl you don't fancy? Third, do you really regard making love to an unconscious body exciting or does the potential pleasure result from feeling freer of anxiety? You say you 'had her at your mercy'. Has sex always been such a dreadful battle for you? And fourth, are you always so tough on your body (and mind) that you see them as tools (or weapons) to be used at whim? If so, I have news. Your central nervous system is not a machine. Male sexual circuitry is actually designed to prevent erection in the absence of positive desire. This was no 'failure'. You simply had no feelings.

Painful penis 1

When I try to masturbate, my foreskin hurts. It won't seem to retract far enough. Doug.

Answer

But does it prevent full erection or not? If it does, you have phimosis (a too-tight foreskin) and the doctor may recommend a simple snip, or full circumcision (a routine and pain-free operation). If it does not, you could have adhesions between penis-crown and foreskin, or a foreskin that has never been stretched. Should you wish to ease it, use baby oil as a lubricant and roll the over-layer downwards with the gentlest of pressures, a little further each time.

Painful penis 2

This October I'm going to Cornwall to stay with my female penfriend whom I met on holiday there when I was thirteen. All my friends at school have hinted I may be expected to sleep with her. This has crossed my mind on several occasions and while I know sex isn't readily available from people you only know from letter-writing, it's occurred to me that should she want me to I can't! The problem is that my foreskin is actually attached to the head of my penis, so I can't pull it back at all without pain (it's impossible when aroused). Please help. Barry.

Answer

This is a straightforward medical problem although the question of whether you should lose your virginity to a penfriend is a matter we'll discuss in a moment. The condition you describe is called phimosis and means a 'too-tight foreskin'. This is simply the 'luck of the draw' – nature has made you that way – and there's no shame or stigma involved. However, there is pain. You ought to be able to retract your foreskin fully, especially when aroused, and also for reasons of hygiene, but in your condition I am sure this would result in the most excruciating discomfort. Clearly if nothing is done it will be a long time before you start to enjoy a proper sexual relationship so can I beg you to get things sorted out now? Ask to see your GP and explain in words of one syllable what seems to be the problem. He or she will refer you to a consultant surgeon who can give you a very simple correctional circumcision. Tell yourself thousands of men get this trouble each year, they have the op and enjoy trouble-free lives therefter. As for your penfriend, bear in mind your mates at school are teasing you and it's best to count on nobody's favours in advance. You'll be ready to make love to someone when you feel so close it seems like a natural (and less intimidating) step forward.

Illegal sex

I'm a nineteen-year-old man. I recently met and went to

bed with the daughter of an old family friend. I thought she was my age but afterwards she revealed she was only fifteen and could have me sent to prison for illegal sex. She keeps ringing and asking for things, including more sex and money. Damion.

Answer

Although you are technically and legally in the wrong, blackmail is also a crime. I suggest you tape-record this woman's demands, then use this to negotiate a truce. Meanwhile, learn from experience that a woman may be younger than she looks.

Late puberty

I read last week about a boy going through puberty at thirteen. Well, I am now sixteen and have had erections since I was about ten, yet I still have no pubic hair, nor have I reached puberty. My friends boast they started when they were eight or nine years old. My mum told me puberty happens to boys between the ages of eleven and sixteen. I'm really worried something may be wrong with my body. Phil.

Answer

Relax – your mum is right, and your friends are exaggerating. On average, male puberty starts at around twelve and continues till a boy is about seventeen. If you want to know more, have a word with your doctor next time you visit the surgery, or you can get a booklet for £1.50 called *How Your Body Changes* from the Family Planning Association, 27-35 Mortimer Street, London W1N 7RJ (tel. 071-636 7866). By the way, newborn babies can have erections – this is nothing to do with puberty.

Not yet developed

I am a boy of nearly sixteen and I have no hair where I should have. My penis is only two inches long. I'm really ashamed to go in the showers in school because they call me names like maggot dick and baldy. I'm currently going out with a girl. She wants to play with my penis and go all the way with me. Is there some sort of medication I could buy to help my hair grow? Please help me. I'm desperate. Euan.

Answer

As you can see from other answers, puberty may start as late as sixteen or seventeen, and there's no patent hair-tonic so you've just got to be patient. If you're really worried, have a private chat with your doctor. I know the other kids tease you rotten and at times you could cheerfully kill them. But no girl is going to stop touching you just because you're not very hairy. She isn't after hair.

Hairy problem 1

I have a serious problem with hair. I am only twelve but I have a moustache and am getting a beard. I also have a lot of hair on my legs, arms, hands, chest, toes and even knuckles. None of my friends have any hair, facial or otherwise. Should I shave? I tried once but messed it up and it looked really obvious. Everyone teased me. Is there any medication I could take to stop the hair growing? Could I use hair remover? PS. I am a boy. From Desperate.

Answer

Over the next few years, all your male classmates will grow body and facial hair just like you. I know it's a bit awkward being the 'first' but you could also take pride in it. Yes, shaving is fine but I should get your dad or an uncle (or the barber) to show you how!

Hairy problem 2

I'm a twelve-year-old boy and people say I'm mature for my age. I've developed hair at the base of my penis. In the showers at PE I've noticed that none of the other boys have this problem. My friend says I might have started puberty. Please help. I'm beginning to want to cut some of the hair off. Anon.

Answer

You've certainly started puberty and there's absolutely no reason to be ashamed. You could even try feeling proud of this! I'm sure some of the other boys are a little envious. The hair is normal and will also appear under your arms and (eventually) on your chin (where it's called a beard!).

Erections again

I'm a thirteen-year-old boy but have a bad problem. I get erections, not just one, but up to ten a day. Is this normal? I'm so depressed about it.

Answer

Yes, it's quite normal. When you go into puberty all these new sex hormones flood round your body. You'd be more worried, in fact, if things weren't working properly. Over the next few months, it will happen less. Meanwhile when you're walking cover the worst of your embarrassment with your hands or a school bag.

Masturbation disgust

I feel so disgusted after I masturbate. I try not to do it but it's hard. The longest I've gone without doing it is ten days. Is masturbation normal for a boy of fourteen? Can you help me to stop myself before I do it? Ian.

Answer

Masturbation is a natural, if not central, part of your sex life, especially during teenage when you need to understand and discover your growing body and feelings. It's practically universal among fourteen-year-old boys and there's absolutely no reason to feel disgusted with yourself.

Older problem

I'm eighteen and have recently taken my relationship with my partner into a sexual dimension. The second time, all was going well when I lost my erection. The problem is the condom. Putting this on interferes with my sexual momentum and destroys spontaneity. Greg.

Answer

It really needn't. All you have to do is make the donning of the condom a natural and exciting part of foreplay. So when you've undressed, and hands begin to sneak towards genitals, get her to roll the friendly rubber sheath slowly down your penis. Allow her to spend several minutes over this. After the first few seconds, I suspect you'll begin to forget you're even wearing protection, so much will pleasure rule your thoughts. Subtle hint: unwrap the condom and place it somewhere handy under the bed before you get undressed.

Upright penis

Ever since I've been able to get an erection in my penis, something tells me it's not quite normal as it stands vertical at about 6 inches high when I'm standing up. Sex doesn't seem possible with it like this and adult films I've seen show other men's penises just standing horizontally away from their bodies. What's wrong with me?

Answer

Men do stand to attention at different angles but mostly with their parts pointing upwards. Nature intended this because the woman's vagina also slopes upwards thereby assisting the most common lovemaking position (face-to-face).

Condom query 1

I'm a ten-year-old boy and I found a packet of condoms in the bathroom. I told my older friends and they burst into laughter and made funny jokes about them which I didn't understand. What do they do? Are they dangerous? Do they hurt? Where do you put them? Can I use them? Pete.

Answer

Condoms are rubber sheaths that fit over the penis during sex. They are intended to stop girls getting pregnant and prevent infections from passing between two people. Far from being dangerous (unless you're silly enough to put one on your head) they can save lives. You don't need to use them until you're old enough to make love but there's nothing wrong with taking a good look at them in private. Your friends are laughing from embarrassment, that's all.

Condom query 2

I've had a relationship with a girl for some time. I'm very keen on her. The problem is that we want to have sex, but when I try condoms on my penis they are all too big. I'm sixteen. Gary, Newcastle. PS: I enclose an accurate picture of the problem.

Answer

Condoms do come in different sizes and they are available *free* from the Family Planning Association. Look up your nearest branch in the phone book.

Foot fetish?

My problem is that I keep having fantasies about girls wearing tights, especially brown, black or white ones. I have been caught at school staring at girls in tights and now it has spread around the school and I'm getting teased a lot. This obsession is ruining my life. Please help. Bryan, aged eleven.

Answer

Bryan, it's very common for boys to look at girls' legs and get interested in what they wear. Don't respond to the teasing – you're not peculiar.

Penis concern

I'm a boy of thirteen and I'm particularly worried about a part of my body. On my penis I have two veins which start at the top of my penis and finish at the beginning of my testicles. These veins stick out a lot. Am I abnormal and can I do anything about it? Darren.

Answer

These veins have to work very hard and need to be thick to carry the blood swiftly round this part of your anatomy. All men have them.

Is circumcised

I'm writing to you because I don't know who else to turn to. I'm very depressed and embarrassed. When I was younger I was circumcised. I don't know why because I'm not Jewish and I'm too embarrassed to ask my parents why. When I was younger I thought I was somehow deformed but now I think I understand. I'm fourteen years old. Is it safe to have sex without a foreskin? Charles.

Answer

Not only is it safe to have sex without a foreskin, lots of people prefer it! There's no need to feel concerned.

Penis problem

I have a problem and it scares me a lot. It's my penis. I can't tell anyone. There's a skin forming from my skin to the middle of my penis head and I'm scared it's wrong. From a very scared boy.

Answer

This is called the frenum or frenulum. It's shaped a bit like the skin under your tongue at the bottom of your mouth. Every male has one and the skin can be especially sensitive.

Masturbation again and again

I'm a fourteen-year-old male. I masturbate every night and always ejaculate. I need to know:
a) Can this ruin my health?
b) Can I run out of sperm?
c) When I provide a urine sample for my school medical, might my masturbation show up? Evan.

Answer

a) No. b) Yes in the sense that if you masturbate five or six times in a row, you will eventually have a 'dry' orgasm but it doesn't matter (it can be fun) and the sperm will be fully replenished by your testes within a couple of days. c) No.

Large breasts

I have a big problem and hope you can help. I'm a boy of eleven and I've got large breasts. When I go swimming with school I get teased. I try to ignore my classmates but I get very upset. My doctor says I need to lose weight and do exercise. I hardly eat anything now. Please can you tell me what to say back to the people who tease. A desperate boy. Duncan.

Answer

If you get fat, you will get fat everywhere, including on

your chest. What you need to do is lose weight over the next couple of years by gradually changing your diet towards lower-fat, non-sugary foods and by taking up some form of exercise that you enjoy. Even ten-pin bowling will do, so long as you *move*. What you say to the kids who tease you is *nothing* – smile and let them get tired.

Want to strip

We are two teenage boys who desperately need help. We really want to become male strippers just like the Chippendales and Dreamboys etc. Whenever we mention this to our parents, or friends, they just laugh and think we're joking. We both think we've got fairly good looks and bodies and every night lift weights. We regularly visit the gym to help us on the road to success. We aren't shy about it; we just don't get any support. We both have girlfriends, so we're OK in that department (you see we're attractive to some girls). If we did pursue this career, would it mean giving up others – eg. we both hope to go to college? It may sound stupid, but we need help. Ron and Joe.

Answer

There's no real conflict between going to college and pursuing a flamboyant career in showbusiness. People will grin a bit but you'll have to put up with worse on stage!

Wants a better body

I'm a fifteen-year-old boy and have been doing special adbominal exercises since the beginning of the year from a book I sent off for. It guarantees a 'Chippendale-style' body within six months and 'noticeable results' after the first few weeks. So far, I haven't noticed any results. I wanted to get mature girls to ask me out because I'm sick of fourteen-year-olds but nothing's happened. Andy.

Answer

First, ask for your money back. Second, realize that a Chippendale-style body is yours only after extensive weight-training, usually at a professional gym. Third, girls don't ask bodies out, they want dates with people. You'd do better to learn how to make good conversation.

Lads and nipples

I'm a lad of sixteen and my nipples are soft. When I get in a cold shower they go normal and hard. I'm so embarrassed to go to places like the swimming baths. Can I make them normal again without having a shower all the time? Anthony.

Answer

Well, there's nothing wrong with them. Nipples only *go* hard when you're excited or cold. You've been watching too many Schwarzenegger movies. Men aren't really made of metal.

3

Girls' Bodies

For girls, puberty can start even earlier than in boys – at eight or nine. As a result, some girls sadly get pregnant at ten though no person of this age is really in a position to cope with motherhood. This chapter is specially about girls' bodies and the great changes that occur as womanhood begins. The questions are very precise – such as size and shape of breasts and growth of body hair. Like boys, girls can suffer agonies about the different rates at which development occurs

Going through changes

I'm an eleven-year-old girl (soon to be twelve) and I don't know how to talk to my mum about periods or about any other things about the facts of life. I want to start my periods and wear a bra, but I get all shy. Please can you send me some fact sheets about the changes that we have to go through? A friend at school started wearing a bra the other day and I feel left out. I really want a bra and can't pluck up the courage to ask for one. None of the other girls in my class seem to worry about asking their parents for these things. From Anon.

Answer

But they do, as my postbag makes clear. I'm sure if you screw up your courage, you could ask Mum – she has periods too, remember. Failing that, could you talk to an auntie or a teacher at school? If you want a copy of my free leaflet on starting periods, just write to Phillip Hodson Factsheet, Code PHFS, Tambrands Ltd, Dunsbury Way, Havant, Hampshire, PO9 5DG.

Early developer

Please help. My breasts are big. Everybody stares and laughs at me. I'm the only girl in my class that wears a bra (I'm nearly nine). Is there something wrong with me? Please answer – I am deeply distressed. Gwen.

Answer

It's really tough to get teased for being absolutely normal. But some girls do start their periods at the age of eight or nine. To make it more difficult, breasts start to grow even before you get your periods. Tell yourself there are pluses and minuses. First, you are well. You are maturing before the rest. You can be sure of having a figure. You will not be so disturbed by your body as a teenager (since you are going through the changes now). On the other hand, it is inevitable that some people will makes jokes *so be prepared for this*. Say 'I've heard it all before' over and over to yourself. Also tell yourself that people who tease are *always anxious*. In your case, they are secretly envious of what you've got and they want.

Hasn't yet developed

I need help. I'm very worried. I'm going to be twelve soon and the problem is I haven't developed at all. I have hardly any pubic hairs and I'm very flat-chested. All my friends and people in the year I'm in have developed or started. Am I just unusual? Please help as I'm worried. Paula.

Answer

You're not unusual in developing a bit later than some girls in your class. Puberty starts at any time between the ages of nine and sixteen. Everyone has pubic hair by the age of seventeen but not everyone gets the same amount of hair or a bust of the same size. And we'd all look pretty silly if we did!

Big bust

I'm a pretty sixteen-year-old with big breasts. Recently, I've started work experience where I'm surrounded by many male workers. Because of the size of my bust, I decided to cover up so nobody would get the wrong idea. This was OK until one afternoon it got too hot and I went into the spare office to remove my bra. When I came back, many of the men made sexual remarks and tried to get close to me. Instead of being annoyed, this seemed to excite me and I noticed my nipples were erect and sticking through my shirt. Help me – am I normal for reacting like this and should my nipples go hard? Sheena.

Answer

Not everyone likes being ogled and no one wants to be

harassed but you obviously responded to this attention (though there are other ways to get it). Nipples naturally go hard when you are excited, aroused, frightened or cold, but I don't think you were cold.

Large breasts and more

I'm thirteen years old and fed up with myself. My boobs are the biggest in the class and the boys keep pinging my bra strap in assembly and making jokes about me. When we have gym they all watch to see my boobs go up and down and it's very embarrassing. At home, even my dad and brother pass rude remarks. Why do they all do this? Also, my girlfriend says that the brown marks at the top of my legs mean I've had sex. Is this true? Gaynor.

Answer

No – you know it isn't true because you know you haven't had sex! Brown marks are just brown marks. Your friend is teasing you. The males have a go because they're embarrassed. Tell them to push off – they'll grow up eventually. As time goes by, other girls will also develop and you'll soon stop feeling the odd one out.

Large breasts again

At school when we have a shower all the girls stare at me because I have a big bust. I'm ten, fat and I'm a size 40 bust. I get teased about this. I'm also a slow person at everything and everyone calls me dimmie and fat cow. This upsets me. Jean.

Answer

I think you're saying you feel self-conscious about your body in general. Obviously if you're a large size, your 'vital statistics' will also be big. Plus, if you're heavy, it's difficult to move quickly. Now – you can try to eat healthy food as part of a slimming plan. But weight-loss should only be attempted slowly over a few months – crash diets are bad for you and you end up gaining it all back anyway. And you should always feel entitled to be yourself. If people object to your appearance that is *their* problem and *their* stupidity. Some of the world's greatest artists, writers, thinkers, musicians and athletes have been very big and very heavy.

Flat-chested

I'm thirteen and I have no bust at all! None whatsoever. I told my mum and she told me to do some bust-increasing exercises. The boys at school really pick on me saying, 'You're so flat you make a wall look bulgy.' It really hurts. I'm thinking of talking to my mum again but I know what the answer will be. And she'll tell everyone and they'll have a good laugh and make snide remarks about me. Please help, I'm desperate. Vicky.

Answer

Breasts aren't muscles so exercise cannot make them any bigger. I know it feels unfair, but puberty for girls can start as late as sixteen or seventeen so you *have* to be patient. Tell the lads to go and find a brain and share it out between them.

Really flat-chested

I'm fifteen and totally flat-chested. I mean really flat. I'm not even budding. You can't tell the difference between my breasts and my stomach! They are not tender like most teenage girls' breasts and it's really getting me down. I can't go swimming any more and dread the summer with those short and skimpy tops! I've tried exercises and everything. Please don't advise me to go to my doctor or to talk to my mother as I find the situation too embarrassing. Nessa.

Answer

But your mum may have the answer. If she was a late developer, or has a small bust, the chances are you'll be the same. Some girls don't start puberty till sixteen or seventeen – some girls always look like Kate Moss. I know you feel left out but what really matters is being a strong, healthy woman on the inside. People are *not* their chests. If your mum's small on top, she can also tell you how she coped.

Flat-chested again

I hope you can help me. I am twelve and my breasts are completely flat. I look just like a boy and I am called 'pavement slab' and 'ruler'. I feel upset and alone about this because I don't think anyone else in my year has this problem. Please help. Deirdre.

Answer

They do, as you can see from the letters above. It's early days yet – wait and see.

Painful breasts

I'm eleven years old and having trouble with my breasts. They're giving me aches and pains. Mostly when someone knocks me there and when I lie on my front in bed. I've got lots of friends but because of this I feel like hiding away in the corner. Would you advise me to go to the doctor or should I just wait for it to go away? Doreen.

Answer

Your doctor would always be happy to see you but this sounds like a 'growing pain'. The first sign of puberty for girls is swelling of the breasts which can feel super-sensitive. But there's no need to become a hermit – just lie down with a hot-water bottle when it's really bad.

Weighty problem

My boobs flop up and down when I play volley-ball but my mother won't let me have a bra. All the boys in school make fun of me – what can I do? Barbara.

Answer

Demonstrate the problem, either by running up and down on the spot in front of your mother, or by asking her to come and watch you at school. If paying for the bra is an issue, offer to find the cash yourself from the proceeds of birthdays or some Saturday job. If all else fails, button-hole a favourite female teacher, unload the problem on her and plead with her to tackle your mum. Whether there is a real need (because your breasts are weighty) or quite simply because you would feel better in a bra, you ought to be able to get one.

Breast milk

When do you get milk in your breasts? We are three worried eleven-year-old girls who are scared that when we have a baby, we might not have any milk to feed them. Anon.

Answer

You get milk in your breasts automatically after giving birth to a baby. There are sometimes problems in breastfeeding but rarely with the supply of milk.

No to bra

Please help me. I am thirteen. I have not started my periods but I have pubic hair down below and under my arms and I have a small bust (size 30 inches). However, my mum won't let me wear a bra because she said I am only allowed to wear one when I have started my periods. All the other girls in my class wear one. Sometimes, I get a bit jealous but when I do any running my bust wobbles. Sometimes I have to stop because it hurts and feels tender. Mary.

Answer

Remind your mum that breasts tend to grow before you start your periods so her rule does sound a little strange. It also makes you feel like the odd one out at school when you need to belong. If she's worried about the cost, tell her you'll help save up the money. But don't panic. From what you've said, your periods are due jolly soon.

Uncomfortable bra

I am twelve years old and in my first year of secondary school. At my last school, the nurse told us we should start wearing a bra as soon as possible. My mum bought me a bra and I've tried to wear it and it's comfortable at first, but then it starts getting itchy and I take it off. I told my mum this but she just said, 'It's the most comfortable one available so you'd better get used to wearing it!' But I can't. Then a friend said I should wait till I'm older before I wear it. Now I don't know what to do. Brenda, Essex.

Answer

The most important information is missing. You don't tell me the size of this problem. If your boobs are big, then a bra will give you the necessary support. However, the fact is that some women go right through life quite happily never wearing or needing to buy one. I guess you are at a stage where your chest is also very sensitive to the slightest touch from tight clothing. Since this irritability will lessen as you develop, perhaps it would be best to wait a bit longer.

Wants a bra

I think I need a bra but I'm not sure how to ask my mum for one. I think if I ask her she will laugh and say I'm being silly. Kirstie.

Answer

Then get your argument ready. Tell her that you may not be big-chested, but other reasons exist for wearing bras. Such as wanting to look like the other girls. Such as not being teased because you haven't got one. Such as wanting one because you want one (where's the harm, anyway?). My challenge to you is this. If you're grown up enough to wear a woman's clothes, you've got to be grown up enough to argue and reason to get them. So take the risk and defend your corner. Mum will have to agree one day.

Embarrassed about bra

I've got a problem. I'm only ten years old but my breasts have already started to develop. At school we do a lot of PE and I just wear shorts and a T-shirt. I wear a bra but I take it off in PE in case the boys find out. The other day a boy stole it from my bag and ran around the classroom waving it. I'm so embarrassed. What can I do? Nicky.

Answer

Try to ignore him. If he persists, accuse him of wearing women's clothing.

Breast cancer worry

I'm ten years old and my right breast has a tiny lump in it. You can't see it but it throbs a tiny bit when you press it. I haven't told anyone because it's embarrassing. I've had it about a month and I'm a bit concerned. From Emma.

Answer

You could always see your GP if you're very worried but it's quite normal to have little breast lumps at your age. Think of them as 'buds' that turn into your breasts.

Nipple hair

I'm a fifteen-year-old girl and have a dark hair growing from one of my nipples. Is this common? I'm worried about it and too embarrassed to ask anyone. Pam.

Answer

Yes, and some people think it's quite attractive. If you're really bothered (and it's not growing from a mole) you could always pluck it out.

Inverted nipples

I'm a fifteen-year-old girl who has a very embarrassing problem. My breasts are developing well but my nipples seem peculiar. They only appear if I touch them or if I have nothing on. When I'm wearing my bra or bikini-top they disappear and my boobs look very strange. I don't stand staring at other girls' breasts but I do notice I'm different from the others. What can the matter be? Roseanna.

Answer

Nothing's wrong, you simply have 'inverted' nipples. Some girls in your school will be the same so don't imagine you're the only one. Your nipples will generally perk up if you get excited or shiver – and there should be no problem later on if you ever want to breast-feed.

Inverted nipples 2

My problem is that I have inverted nipples. I'm fourteen years old, weigh eight stone and I'm 5 foot 6 inches tall.

I'd so much love to be a model, but I find that this would stand in my way because I'd like to do topless modelling. I'd be grateful if you could let me know where to go or what to do to get some help. Yasmin.

Answer

Unless your nipples 'pop up' when you touch them with an ice cube, there's not much you can do – short of drastic and perhaps risky surgery. I'd try fashion rather than glamour modelling.

Nipple knowledge

Please help me, Phillip. The problem is my breasts are growing but the nipples aren't. Sometimes when I wake up, one of my nipples has got little lumps on and the other hasn't. It doesn't hurt and they soon disappear. Please help because I am really scared. Fiona, aged thirteen.

Answer

I am really glad to be able to tell you that everything is normal. These little bumps only appear when you get a bit chilly or excited. Maybe you have really interesting dreams! One female breast is never truly identical to the other. It may be larger or smaller, lean to left or right or have slightly different skin. It may also respond more to cold or warmth. Nipples also vary. Some people have pointy ones; others have 'inverted' ones which only show up when someone gives you a thrill or chucks a bucket of water over you. Some people even have more than one set of nipples, but I think that's quite enough breast talk for now.

Babies for boys

I really hope you can answer my question: Why can't boys have babies? I like babies but don't like how they come. I want boys to have them. It can't be impossible, because nothing's impossible. Also, if you have a healthy baby, what must you eat and drink? Davina.

Answer

Boys can't have babies because their bodies are the wrong shape inside. They can't make a nest for the egg, they can't supply food for it and they cannot move their bones to allow space for a birth. It's not true that everything is possible, though some scientists believe a man could carry a baby in his body for a couple of months if a woman donated a fertilized egg. I hear *you* saying you are a bit afraid of giving birth. Well, it doesn't have to happen *unless* you want it to. And it doesn't have to happen *until* you want it to. By the time you are ready to have children of your own (or not), lots of people will have helped you come to terms with these feelings. PS: pregnant mums can eat more or less what they want but they shouldn't smoke or drink alcohol.

Pillow talk

I am a very worried fourteen-year-old girl. The problem is that I like to hug my pillow with my body at night. I have tried to stop doing it but cannot. Please help. Basically all I want to know is if I have harmed my body in any way? Louise.

Answer

Pillows are only dangerous if they obstruct your breathing. And it's completely natural to want to cuddle or hug something when you try to sleep. So you can stop worrying.

Wants someone to love

Every time I watch TV and I see someone kissing, I pretend it's me. Sometimes when I'm about to go to bed and I've finished brushing my teeth, I turn off the lights and I kiss the reflection of me in the mirror. Then at night I roll up my sheets and pretend I'm having hugs with 'him'. Please can you tell me what to do about this? I'm eleven years old and want to kiss just about everybody. Gina.

Answer

Try not to feel guilty – this sounds like normal growing up. Most people put huge posters of their favourites on their bedroom walls for the same reason – they like what they see. They even kiss them! Eventually, you'll realize you want a close *live* friend of your own.

I love my teddy bear

I'm a twelve-year-old girl and I don't know what's wrong with me. I get this funny feeling in my tummy and I go upstairs, grab a teddy and pretend I'm in love with it. I stop when I get this tingling sensation, then it just goes and I forget about it until I get it again. Please tell me why I do this and what is wrong with me. Alice.

Answer

There's nothing wrong with you except raging hormones. Puberty is making your body wake up to adult feelings of desire.

Sexual feelings

I've been having funny feelings when watching sex on TV and I've wondered what these feelings were. I asked my school nurse and she said they were sexual feelings and I should tell my parents, but I haven't got the guts. What do you think I should do? I'm really worried about myself. Grace.

Answer

I'd ask the school nurse to get hold of a pamphlet called 'How your body changes' from the Family Planning Association and let you read it. Then you could talk to anyone about this with confidence because you'd already know the basics. But these feelings are normal – you don't have to 'confess'.

Exciting feeling

When I see older men my vagina starts tingling. It can be hard to stop myself blushing and it's hard not to scratch it. My friends have noticed but I can't tell them because they would laugh. Is this normal? I'm eleven years old. Melanie.

Answer

Yes – your brain is sending a sexual message down your spine to your newly active vagina. You'll gradually get used to it – even enjoy it.

Sweat, sweat sweat

Please could you put me out of my embarrassing situation? It is that I sweat a lot. It's not only smelly at times, but it also seeps through all my clothes. I do use an anti-perspirant deodorant and I also wash under my arms. The deodorant does take the smell away but the seeping continues. Please print this letter as I'm sure other girls have this problem. Sally, West Sussex.

Answer

Of course, and it's not only girls who worry. The problem can affect anyone. Worse still, worrying about it can actually make you sweat *more* because anxiety stimulates your sweat glands. Let's agree that sweating is normal. You get rid of up to two litres of water every day from your body, much of it by sweating. It happens when you get tense and it happens in order to cool down your skin. If you are very fat or drink too much tea, coffee and coke containing caffeine you will sweat most. So deal with this yourself by adjusting your eating and drinking. If you wear plastic or nylon clothes, your sweat will make more mess, so try to get cotton underwear and shirts. If the problem is really big (and I mean enormous) see your doc, 'cos they have remedies that help. But so long as you wash, and change your underclothes *daily*, the smell should offend no one. Fresh sweat is actually a turn-on. (It's only 24 hours later that we begin to hold our noses.)

Masturbation

My boyfriend asked if I masturbated and I felt a fool

because I didn't know how to. How old should you be to do it? Julia.

Answer

There are no ages, and there are no 'shoulds'. You can masturbate at any time of life, or not, depending on your feelings and beliefs. There are some women who never masturbate because they didn't discover it before having a boyfriend and possibly don't feel the need afterwards. Other women first played with themselves during childhood, while many only experiment in their teens. Women tend to do it later, and less, than men, partly because their sex organs are more hidden (not 'to hand') and partly because of double standards suggesting that what is normal for boys is dirty for girls. One famous writer (George Bernard Shaw) said 'Ninety-nine per cent of people masturbate and one per cent are liars.'

Scared of dying

I'm very scared because recently I've heard on telly that you can die from masturbating. I've been masturbating since I was six, even though I didn't realize it at first. I'm now twelve. Can I die? Also, if you have sex before you have ever, ever, ever had your period, can you have children when you are older? If it is true, then is it the same with masturbation? Debbie.

Answer

Masturbation *cannot* kill you unless you do it while jumping off a cliff. Nor will it stop you having babies later on. Nor would having sex before you start your periods stop you having babies later on though you'd be too young to cope with it.

More masturbation

Please help me. I know it sounds disgusting but sometimes I give myself sexual pleasure. I was wondering if it would stop me from having children when I'm older. I've tried to stop. Is there something wrong with me? Della.

Answer

Absolutely not.

Masturbation again

I have an embarrassing urge. Every so often I have urges to lie on my bed with no clothes on. Am I sick-minded? I would *never ever* do it in front of anyone. Can you tell me if this is wrong? If so, how can I stop doing it? I'm eleven years old and I'm a girl. Sylvia.

Answer

You're not sick-minded. You are either feeling sexy or too hot.

Masturbation concerns

Please help. When I was seven a boy of eight put his hands in my knickers and rubbed my vagina. It felt lovely. He did it every day for six weeks. When he stopped, I started myself. I'm twelve now and have been doing it ever since. I'm worried because some people have caught me doing it. Please tell me what it is that I'm doing and why I do it. From Anon.

Answer

It's called masturbation – see the letters above. Usually this is a private activity so don't let anyone push you into it.

Further masturbation concerns

Last year my mother bought me a draught excluder because my bedroom gets very cold at night. I feel very lonely, as if I need a boyfriend. So I take my clothes off and pretend to have sex with it. This leaves my vagina very dry and sweaty. I know this may be dangerous but it feels comfortable. I want to know if it will stop my periods. I'm too shy to talk to my mum about this. Can you help? Angela, aged thirteen.

Answer

Touching yourself is harmless. Using household objects to get pleasure won't stop your periods but might cause physical damage if there are rough or dirty edges. Better to use your hands.

Where's my clitoris?

Help! After reading a sex education book I've tried to find my clitoris but it doesn't seem to be there. Daisy.

Answer

It is, but may be hidden in the upper folds of your vaginal lips. Size may also vary from a few millimetres to a centimetre. A good flashlight and mirror should reveal all.

Hymen worries

I'm a thirteen-year-old girl who's recently been in sex education classes at school. During one of these lessons they told us that a woman's hymen breaks before puberty and sometimes for some people it breaks when they first have sex. But I'm really confused. I read a book written by a doctor which said that your hymen is your virginity and it only breaks when you have sex. I don't know what to believe. I've discovered my hymen is broken but I haven't had sexual intercourse or been sexually abused before. My dad keeps saying that a man doesn't want a woman who isn't a virgin. Even though my hymen is broken, am I still a virgin? Wendy.

Answer

Because your hymen can break at any old time, the true modern definition of a virgin is 'one who has never had sexual intercourse'. Although I understand what your dad's saying, most brides in Britain these days are *not* virgins of either sort.

Name-calling

I'm a thirteen-year-old girl and I hate my name – Virginia – because I get teased. My mum thinks it's a lovely name because it belonged to her favourite aunt. Help.

Answer

We can all guess what they call you and it's very b-o-r-i-n-g of them. You can't stop people wasting their time like this but you can alter or shorten your name. Lots of people hate their Christian names – I'm not mad about Phillip which was my gran's surname but I could always ask my friends to call me Phil or even Ian, which is my middle name. You could be Ginny, or Gina or plain Vee. Mum doesn't have to be upset because for the family, and legally, you can remain Virginia.

Hygiene

I'm very worried about my friend. She keeps on licking her fingers and then putting her fingers in unnecessary places on her body. I'm wondering whether she will get a horrible disease because after she puts them there she licks her fingers again. Please help. Liz.

Answer

It depends what she's touching. The vagina is self-cleansing – the bottom isn't. The reason we need to 'wash our hands after going to the toilet' is to stop germs called bacteria from getting into our tummies where they can cause pain, fever and diarrhoea. It's not because 'parents are fusspots'.

Baby blues

I'm desperate to have a baby! When one of the girls in my favourite TV soap found out that she was pregnant, I was green with envy. I'm totally desperate, but my age is a problem. I'm eleven years old. Am I going crazy? Polly.

Answer

No, it's natural to become broody when your body goes into puberty. Even more so when the star of your favourite soap gives birth. However, this woman is twice your age with a husband and experience to help her cope. Enjoy this feeling as a 'rehearsal' for later on because, believe me, you *don't* want a baby now. You've got nowhere to put one!

Vibrator worries

My problem is that about five years ago my brother's mate made me use a body massager to make me orgasm while he watched. Since then I keep going numb and tingling down there. I've been to my doctor and he says it's nerves but I'm worried it's more serious. Please, please help. Pauline.

Answer

It's a combination of two things. First you feel guilty anyway because you know your brother's mate was out of order. Second, when you feel sexy in this part of your body it reminds you of the guilt. But believe the doctor – having an orgasm *is* physically harmless.

Miscarriage

I'm fifteen years old and haven't long come out of hospital over a miscarriage. I'm starting to feel bad because I think I could have caused it. I cry because I can't believe I was going to have a baby, even though I know I was too young anyway. It was a girl. I really love kids. Now I keep thinking I won't ever be able to have one – that they'll keep dying inside me. Shirley.

Answer

Hey – it's natural to grieve when you lose a baby whatever happened during the pregnancy. What you need to do is remember her – this was a real person who really died. Why not give her a name and write down all you hoped she'd grow up to be? The Miscarriage Association, Clayton Hospital, Wakefield, West Yorkshire, WF1 3JS can give you further help if you drop them a line.

Pubic hair colour

I'm eleven years old. Some of my friends say I'll get blonde pubic hair because I have blonde hair. Some say I'll get black or brown pubic hair. What's the right answer? Tracey.

Answer

Most of the time the pubic hair is the same colour as the hair on the head, only a shade or two darker. This is because the hair on your head is exposed to the sun which lightens it.

All in a tangle

I'm eleven years old and my pubic hairs are beginning to show. But they keep getting tangled. It's very uncomfortable. I keep wanting to scratch them. I don't have anyone to talk to because my mum doesn't talk to me about things like that. Do other people have the same problem? From a distressed anonymous reader.

Answer

We *all* have this problem and sometimes you do have to sort them out a bit. You may also be extra sensitive while your 'changes' are happening.

Trimmed pubic hairs

I'm fourteen years old and I recently shaved my vaginal hairs and I'm worried they won't come back. Tiny red spots have appeared and it's very itchy and rough. Please give me some advice. From Anon.

Answer

Worry not – the red bumps *are* the hairs growing again.

Shaving embarrassment

I am eleven and a half years old and everyone at school – well, all my friends – have shaved their legs and they said why don't *you* do it? I said no, because it's silly. And my friends called me a baby, so I did shave my legs. I told my mum and she went mad. Then she said not to do it again. I felt so embarrassed. I ran upstairs and daren't show my face. What will I do? PS: Please print my letter because I need your help and I think your advice page is good and I think you should make it bigger. Julie.

Answer

Thanks for the plug – it worked. I think everyone is getting things out of proportion – you, your friends and even your mum. We are talking about a few hairs on your legs not nuclear war. Everyone's entitled to their view. If your mates feel grown-up with smooth legs, fine. If you think it's a waste of time, stick to your guns, though tell the others you can sort of see why they want to do it. As for your mum, she clearly does not feel too comfortable with your looming teenage. Shaving does not do any damage; nor will it mean the hair grows back tougher. It's just a bore to have to keep doing it. So if she goes on about it, ask her … well … to keep her hair on! PS: you can buy special hair-removing creams or even cosmetic sandpaper(!) from the chemist.

Underarm hair

We have a friend and we feel very embarrassed for her. We go swimming a lot together and she never shaves under her arms. We're not sure whether or not to mention it to her. Should we? From two anonymous girls.

Answer

Why not let her make her own mind up? Some women shave and that's fine. Some women prefer the natural look and that's also fine.

Moustache problem

Help! I've got a sort of moustache like a man's but I am a girl aged eleven. People are always laughing and talking about me because I have it. Can I get rid of it? Glenda.

Answer

You can disguise it by using a product like Jolen from the chemist. When you're older, you can have electrolysis to remove it permanently, or ask the doctor about a product called Dianette.

Feeling sexy

My problem is that every four or five weeks I get a funny feeling and all I can think of is boys, kissing and sex. This lasts for about two days. Then immediately afterwards I think boys are the worst thing on earth and I think that sex is disgusting. I've heard that boys get 'wet dreams'. Is this something that girls get, or is it just me? I'm eleven years old and I haven't started my puberty yet, but I'm an early developer.

Answer

It sounds as though you're already getting a monthly surge of hormones which have the effect of making you feel very sexy. It's not like having an orgasm at night – more like getting rather hot for a couple of days. Don't worry, you'll adjust and calm down.

Large nose

I'm twelve years old and I really like this boy at school. The problem is he doesn't like me, probably because I've got an extra-large nose and everybody will hassle him if he goes out with me. All the boys hate the way I look. Pat.

Answer

No, you're the one who hates the way you look. Others just tease you occasionally. This boy has the right to say no but never put yourself down. The good news is big noses are getting fashionable – one Paris designer (Gaultier) insists *all* his models should have them.

Oddly shaped?

I have two pieces of skin hanging from my vagina, one is longer than the other. Is this normal? I'm a physically mature fourteen-year-old girl. I have to open these flaps to insert a tampon. I'm worried this may affect me when I have sex later on. Geraldine.

Answer

These are simply your vaginal lips. Some people have big ones, some have small ones.

Discharge dilemma

I am an eleven-year-old girl and whenever I move I feel as though I have wet myself because my knickers feel wet and cold. When I get to the toilet I look at my pants and there are sort of lumps of creamy stuff (which looks a bit like horseradish sauce!) and I don't know what to do about it! I know I should tell my mum but I feel she would just think I want attention. Mandy.

Answer

As soon as you start puberty, it's normal to have 'secretions' from this part of your body. You need to talk to mum since you'll probably want to get some pant-liners and they cost money! However, there's nothing wrong with you – but see the next reply.

Vaginal wetness

I am an eleven-year-old girl who is confused. At school when I talk to my boyfriend, my privates start to tingle. Then when I am on the toilet I notice a creamy white patch on my knickers. Is it because I talk to my boyfriend, or discharge or something else? From Hannah.

Answer

This sounds like sexual excitement – your vagina gets 'wet' because you're turned on.

Worried about thrush

I'm very worried about thrush. Please answer these four questions. 1. What is thrush? 2. How can I catch it? 3. How can I tell I have it? 4. How can I cure it? A worried female.

Answer

Thrush is a very common yeast infection which practically everyone gets at some stage or other. It doesn't have to be sexually transmitted – if you wear trousers that are too tight or nylon pants or take strong antibiotics or even eat too much sugar, you can get it. The condition may be aggravated by the contraceptive pill. If you've got thrush, you'll know – there's usually a lot of itching, odour and discharge. Treatment involves wearing loose clothes, cotton knickers and cutting down on sugar in the diet. You can use Canesten ointment on the affected parts which you can buy without a prescription from the chemist. In extreme cases, you may have to consult your GP.

Masturbation secret

I was sixteen yesterday. I know that it's now legal for me to have sex but when will it be legal for me to masturbate? You see, when I was fourteen my mother caught me doing it with my hairbrush, and she beat me and told me that it's disgusting and that I must never touch myself like that until I'm older or God will punish me and I will go to hell. But I've been doing it in secret often. Why is it so wrong? Please help me.

Answer

It seems wrong to your mother because that's the way she was brought up. Perhaps she's a Catholic who believes sex is only proper if you want to make a baby? Private masturbation has never been against the law, however, and doctors say it's harmless.

4

From Periods to Pregnancy

This chapter is about girls learning to live happily with their menstrual cycle but also what to do if things go wrong. The questions include coping with the first period, using tampons, whether boys can tell if you've started yet, and if any form of sex carries *no* risk of pregancy.

'The demands the baby made came as a shock. I thought it'd be like a doll, a toy. I'd no idea you had to give up everything' – Ceri Evans, mum, aged seventeen, quoted in the *Independent*.

How to tell

I have started my periods but I don't know how to tell my mum because we don't talk about things like this. How can I tell her? Alex.

Answer

Having a first period should be a moment of pride for a girl. It's an event that should build up your self-confidence. So I feel very sad when I hear about mums (and dads) who won't or can't talk about periods, though I realize even grown-ups can feel shy. You could lead round to the subject by asking Mum to buy you a small paperback called *Have You Started Yet?* by Ruth Thomson (published by Piccolo). The title might give her the hint. Failing this, try speaking to someone you feel comfortable with who *does* have periods – such as an older sister, aunt or teacher. Read the book anyway, because it's crammed with helpful advice about dealing with any cramps or backache you might get.

Starting periods

I haven't started my periods yet and I would like to know what the first signs are? I have also had about three lessons on sex education and haven't told my mum. Most of what we were told I already knew from friends but I am getting worried about my periods. Budgie, aged twelve.

Answer

I can see it's all preying on your mind so let me say at once: this is the most natural thing in the world and it happens to every girl including you. Of course you're worried because you don't know what's involved. But when you do, the experience of growing up is really exciting! Periods can start when you're as young as nine or as old as seventeen. But for most girls, it happens between the ages of eleven and thirteen. Soon after your breasts start to grow (and the gap can be quite a few weeks), your body prepares to release its first egg. To look after that egg, a soft landing place is made in the lining of your womb. When you don't get pregnant, this lining isn't needed. So your body sheds it. *This* is what's called a period. In other words, over several days, a small amount of blood flows from your body (a small quantity you can easily spare – less than an eggcupful). There may be a gap of months between your first period and the next, but after a while, you will probably settle to a monthly routine. To absorb the blood, you need special pads or tampons you can buy from chemists or supermarkets. If you get period pains, a hot-water bottle on the tummy is nice. If you need to know more, take courage and talk to your mum. She's had periods for years! If it's still difficult, talk to the school nurse (if you've got one) or a friendly woman teacher. If you want extra help, I've written a factsheet which you can discuss with Mum – or Dad. Just send a stamped s.a.e. to: Phillip Hodson Factsheet, Dept PHFS, Tambrands Ltd, Dunsbury Way, Havant, Hampshire, PO9 5DG.

Period blues

Please help me. I'm really worried. I get very depressed and cry and feel really miserable. Each time gets worse. It doesn't happen very often (about once a month) but when it happens I just go to pieces. It usually lasts for about two or three days. Is this normal and do other people have the same problems? Please tell me I'm not alone. Anne, Derbyshire.

Answer

You're not alone. It sounds as though you have pre-menstrual tension (PMT; or pre-menstrual syndrome – PMS), a problem affecting up to one third of all women in the country. That's why the feelings are monthly, and last two or three days. I suggest you prepare for these times. Take things as easily as possible when the mood starts. Give up tea and coffee while you're down ('cos the caffeine makes things worse). Get some painkillers or vitamin B6 or Feminax capsules or the Efamol Pre-Menstrual Pack from the chemist and see if they help. Try to reduce any outside stress – so if you're having rows with your parents, cool it as much as possible. Take exercise even if you don't feel like it. See your GP if there's no improvement.

Monthly moods

I'm thirteen and I get terrible moods every three or four weeks when I don't feel like being nice to anyone, not even my dog Madge who's my best friend. This upsets me a lot because I don't mean it. I also get cramping pains in my tummy towards the end of every month when I don't want to go to school but my mum makes me. I'm worried I might have an illness that nobody's noticed or a lump in my tummy. Pippa.

Answer

Please don't panic. This sounds like a classic case of period pains with the new hormones in your body giving you a hard time. If you want to be absolutely certain, go and see the doctor but there are also loads of remedies you can try for yourself. When your periods start, a gland in your brain sends out two sets of signals to your ovaries and they send back two different lots to your brain. It's a bit like a railway line with a station at each end. Unfortunately, in these early days, the trains may whizz up and down too fast for your system to cope. Your moods suffer first. One minute you feel fine – the next you might get depressed as a dose of hormone surges through your poor old body which overreacts, or adjusts too slowly. Then at the beginning of your period the cramps can set in. This is because the womb is a very strong muscle (about the size of your clenched fist) and behaves like any other muscle if tensed too quickly – it cramps into spasm. The problem is worse because you can't reach inside yourself to rub it better so you have to use a different approach. Give the mood swings time to settle down – puberty is a major event both mentally and physically. Try the Efamol Pre-Menstrual pack, combining the correct dose of evening primrose oil with vitamin B6, to stabilize your hormones. If you can, use exercise to stop the cramps – perhaps Madge could do with a walk? If not, even standing up and twisting gently from side to side with your arms outstretched can get the blood circulating properly. Don't just lie down in a ball – this makes the cramps worse. If you must lie down, adopt an L-position with your legs in the air against a wall (for about twenty minutes). Do this in private in case your parents think you've begun worshipping the moon. A hot-water bottle on the tummy, or a warm bath afterwards, are also good ideas.

Starting

I'm an eleven-year-old girl who isn't sure what's happening. Yesterday and today I noticed a quite dark brown stain on my knickers. What is it? Have I started my periods? I've seen this before. Please help me! Brenda.

Answer

Yes, it's called a 'show' or early period. Have a good long chat with your mum about what to do.

Just teasing 1

I have just had my first period. I am ten. I am wearing pads. All of my class knows about it and teases me. I need some advice on how to cope with my problem. Kathy. PS: most of the boys tease me about it because they can't have periods.

Answer

Right – they feel awkward, 'funny', and left out. They also feel stupid because they don't understand much about periods. But you know you should be quite proud of growing up, so don't get defensive. Smile at them, look happy because things are going well. When somebody teases you run a picture in your mind of that person going bald or sitting on a drawing pin. It will help you cope. When they say – 'You're having a period!' reply, 'Yes, I am. Isn't it great!'

Just teasing 2

I'm a fourteen-year-old girl from Scotland. I'm being teased. They say that Scottish people don't get their periods. The trouble is I haven't had my period. Please help. I'm desperate. Oonagh.

Answer

But that's not because you're a Scot or there'd be no Scottish babies! It's because people begin their periods at different ages (from as young as nine to as old as seventeen). Even in fuddy-duddy England!

Questions about periods

Can I ask you a few questions that I'm worried about?
1. Do you have to wear towels or tampons during a period?
2. What do you do during swimming?
3. Should you not eat certain things during a period?
Please help. From Angela, confused.

Answer

1. You can wear either – just carry out the instructions on the packet.
2. During swimming, a tampon is ideal – swim all you want. Just change it afterwards.
3. Periods are normal and you can eat what you like. Some people get a sugar craving but it's better for your system to get energy from foods like potatoes rather than from bars of chocolate.

How long to wait

I started my periods six weeks and eight days ago. I haven't had my second period yet. I know it's normal for them to be irregular but just out of curiosity, about how long do you think I could wait? I know there's a very big difference between everyone's cycles. I just wondered. From Barbara.

Answer

The gap between your first and second can be weeks or even months. Your body should then settle down, but not every woman has a routine 28-day cycle. Also, if you're underweight or suddenly lose a lot of weight, your periods can stop altogether and you need to see the doc.

Holiday planning

I am going on holiday with the school and I think my period is due that week. I don't know whether to tell the teacher I am unable to go with them. What should I do? Hilary-Anne.

Answer

There's no reason to cancel. Just tell your mum you're worried about this. Make sure you have the right tampons to take with you. Discuss things with a teacher if you need. But remember that periods don't stop you from moving about. You can go dancing, swimming or (if recent ads are to be believed) you can play football too. Have a great time.

Can I use tampons?

Please could you tell me if it's OK for twelve-year-olds to use tampons? Also I read in a book that when you start your periods your breasts stop growing. Is this true? Worried Welshgirl.

Answer

If you are going to use tampons, it's sensible to ask for the 'mini' size to start with. Both Tampax and Lillets make suitable ones. As for breasts, they *start* growing before your periods come on but certainly continue afterwards. (Otherwise most women would be flatties, wouldn't they?)

Pregnancy worry

I'm a twelve-year-old girl with an eighteen-year-old boyfriend. Recently he asked me to go to an overnight party and I went just to please him as I really love him and wanted to make him happy. All the people were over sixteen so I felt a bit strange. Half-way through the party we began playing Postman's Knock, but instead of sticking to the rules, couples began making out all round the room. I knew what was coming and pretty soon it happened. My boyfriend asked me to go all the way with him – so I did. I couldn't tell if we used protection or not. I haven't started my periods yet and I want to know if you can get pregnant if you haven't started. Please help.

Answer

It's highly unlikely you're pregnant but that's only *one* risk. You didn't have *safe sex* because you can't say if a condom was used. You didn't have *legal sex* because you're not sixteen so your boyfriend could be jailed. You didn't have *happy sex* because you got shamed into it by a grown-up who should never have put you on the spot. Of course it's nice to have a boyfriend and I hope you find a good one soon but this guy loves himself not you.

Birth control

Please help – I would like to know something. If a man and woman made love and the man was on contraception and the woman wasn't, would the woman get pregnant? And if the woman was on the pill and the man was not on anything, will the woman still be pregnant? Frances, aged fourteen.

Answer

The word 'contraception' means 'against birth'. So if the man *or* the woman is on good contraception, the woman should not become pregnant. However, no method of contraception is absolutely perfect so it makes sense to use more than one, say the condom plus a spermicidal cream, both of which you can get from a chemist's.

Condom mishap

You are the only one I can turn to for advice. I'm fifteen years of age and made love with my boyfriend for the first time. He used a condom even though I haven't started my periods yet. After we finished, the condom was lying on the sheet of the bed. He then told me that he thought it had fallen off ten minutes before, during sex. I'm now afraid that there is a chance of me becoming pregnant. Please tell me that I'm wrong. Cissie.

Answer

You could only be pregnant if your periods were *about* to start, so it's not likely. However, to be certain, get a home pregnancy test kit from the chemist. The result comes through in about four minutes. The easiest to use – Predictor – costs a bit so make sure your boyfriend pays his share.

Birth control

I'm a fifteen-year-old girl and I've been going steady with a boy for five and a half months. We're both getting very serious and soon will wish to have sexual intercourse. I've never done it before. He's seventeen years old and has done it. All I ask is when is the best time to do it? He doesn't want to wear a condom and my friends tell me the best time to do it is a week after my periods and others say a week before my period. He isn't pressurizing me, and I'm not scared to do it but the last thing I want is to get pregnant. I really need an adult's advice on this matter and you're the only one I can turn to.

Answer

Sex isn't legal until you're sixteen, so don't rush the gun. Secondly, sex isn't just about 'what he wants' but what you *both* want. It's an intimate choice for two people who feel unavoidably involved. So tell him you won't risk an unwanted pregnancy and that's flat. Ask for contraceptive advice either from your doctor, the Family Planning Clinic or the Brook Advisory Service (their national number is 071-708 1234). In general, there is no 'safest' week because ovulation isn't regular (especially at your age) and sperm can live for up to five days inside you. *So the risk without birth control is never worth it.*

Virgin births?

I'm writing to you for my best friend. We're both fourteen. She has a boyfriend who is fifteen and has been going out with him now for ten weeks. He's lovely. About five weeks ago they were at the pictures and instead of just having his arm round her and kissing her, he put his hand on the outside of her boobs. Soon after that he put his hand up her shirt. After a couple of weeks, they'd go to his house and end up on his bed with only underclothes on. He lies on top of her and puts his against hers and sort of moves up and down. She read that you can get pregnant without doing it properly. Is this true? Bella.

Answer

Devastatingly true, tell 'your friend'. Sperm can enter your vagina even without intercourse if the sexual organs get close enough – as between your best friend and her fella. Please show her this answer and get her to stop.

Pregnancy panic

A month ago while I was on holiday I met this wonderful guy. One night he asked me to go back to his apartment and I agreed. I didn't make love to him and I kept my shorts on because I didn't want to run the risk of getting pregnant. All that we did was mutual masturbation and he ejaculated over me just below my chest. Three days later my period started, which was the day it was meant to but now a month later my period has not started. Is it possible that I am pregnant? If I am pregnant, is it possible to have an abortion without my mum knowing? I have stopped eating properly in the hope that I will miscarry. Geraldine.

Answer

I'm glad to reassure you. This boy did *not* make you pregnant because you had a normal period afterwards. However, worry, flying and not eating can all make periods irregular, or even stop. So tell yourself to eat properly now the panic's over.

How to tell 1

Please help me! My mum is really strict. I had my first period about a year ago and I didn't know how to tell her. I've been getting my friend to get me pads because she has had her period and her mum knows. I can't keep doing this. Please can you help me find a way to tell my mum? Mary.

Answer

Mum may be strict but she can't stop nature taking its course. You're having periods, which she must accept. I don't think she's going to be cross with you – though she may be surprised. Just say it casually – 'By the way, Mum, I've started my periods so can I have some money for tampons?' Her strictness is probably about boys and going out – not about your natural development.

How to tell 2

My best friend started her periods about two months ago, but she hasn't told her parents. I was there once when she tried to tell them, but it all came out wrong. She told her mum that she had started … to tidy her bedroom. Please, please could you give her some advice as to what to say? Nigella.

Answer

Get her to practise on you! Pretend to be her mum and listen carefully while she says, 'Mum, can we have a chat in private? I have an announcement to make' – (deep breath) – 'I've started my periods.' She can also rehearse a bit in front of the mirror – and rehearsal *does* help.

Changing tampons

I have a big problem. I'm thirteen and I started my periods about six months ago. I use sanitary towels. I'd like to use tampons but my mum says that they are unsafe if you don't change them enough. But we wear leotards for PE and pads are noticeable. Most of my friends wear tampons. Please help. Penny.

Answer

There is no physical or medical reason why you cannot wear tampons and the advantages are overwhelming. For instance, tampons can't be detected by curious unlookers. Because they're worn inside, they won't smell and tampons can safely be flushed down the loo unlike towels. Arguments about safety apply to *all* types of sanitary protection. So whatever you wear – tampons, pads or towels – you need to change them regularly. In the case of tampons, the new advice is change them at least every six to eight hours. You can wear tampons overnight provided you use a fresh one at bedtime and change it first thing in the morning. You should also be sure to use the strength of absorbency that suits your flow and *never* wear a tampon when you are not having your period.

Toxic shocks

I am a worried teenager desperate to find out what TSS – Toxic Shock Syndrome – means.

Answer

This is a bacterial infection sometimes linked to the use of tampons and sanitary towels, which in a very few instances may prove life-threatening. However, anyone can get it, including men and non-menstruating women. It's so rare most doctors will never see a case and the fear of TSS is out of all proportion to the facts. Provided you follow rules of hygiene *and carry out the instructions on sanitary protection products*, there's nothing to worry about.

Keeping it private

I'm a thirteen-year-old girl. The other day I got my first period. How do I stop people finding out I'm having a period? A friend's bag was rummaged through by some very immature teenage boys. She ended up being very embarrassed because the boys pulled out her sanitary towels in front of her. How do I stop people, especially boys, finding my sanitary towels? Do I keep them in the packet they were bought in, in my school-bag, or what? My mum won't even talk about it. Anne-Marie.

Answer

The cheapest answer is to use a brown paper bag to keep inside your own schoolbag. Companies like Tampax also supply a neat plastic flip-top holder for two tampons which is free – just write to them. They are also introducing a new range of special 'carrying cases' in other materials.

Periods on holiday

Help! In two weeks I'm going on holiday with some cousins (two boys, one girl). My period is due sometime about now, but the last two periods went on quite long. I've only had three so far. If my period goes into my holiday I won't be able to swim! Should I try using

tampons? And is it true there's a layer of skin to break? I
did try using tampons once before but I couldn't get it
in. Wendy.

Answer

Of course you can swim! A tampon will prevent any
leakage – provided you change it once you get out of
the water. The difficulty you may have had with
insertion is easily answered – you were probably
pushing at the wrong angle! If you look at the diagram
on the tampon leaflet, you'll see your vagina slopes
upwards as well as *inwards*. You also have to insert the
end of the applicator into your vagina before you start
pushing. Get a hand mirror and practise a few times
first. As for 'layers of skin', you're referring to your
hymen which all girls are born with but which usually
breaks of its own accord during bike-riding, climbing
trees, etc. The only reason to worry is if it blocks the
entrance to your vagina or is very tough – then you see
the doc.

Tampax wonder

Everyone in my class keeps on saying 'Tampax' and I
don't know what it is. I know all girls have to wear them
so could you please tell me about them? From Debbie,
aged ten.

Answer

A tampon is a small roll of compressed natural cotton
used to mop up menstrual blood products. There is a
special string stitched right through the tampon so that
once inserted into your vagina, at the correct time of the
month, it may be easily taken out again. Tampax is just
the name of the leading brand.

Vegetarianism and periods

I'm a fourteen-year-old vegetarian and I'd like to know if being a vegetarian will have affected my periods. I've not started my periods yet and I'll be fifteen in the summer. What do you think? Marjorie.

Answer

Provided you eat *enough* food and make sure you get the right vitamins there's nothing to worry about. (Periods become irregular or stop if your weight falls below about 90 pounds).

Painful periods

I'm in desperate need of help. I've just started my period and it hurts awfully. It usually lasts for about a week or more. I can't talk to my mum about it. She doesn't understand my problem and wouldn't listen anyway. I don't have another relative I can talk to, either. You're my last hope. Denise.

Answer

I know you don't feel like it but exercise is the best remedy for period pains. Your womb is a muscle like any other and may get a fit of the cramps. In the first years of puberty, these may be particularly severe because the hormones controlling the womb take a while to settle into balance. You can't reach inside yourself to massage your womb so movement of the whole body (walking, dancing, swimming) is the next best remedy. Failing that, stand up and swing gently in a twisting movement from side to side for about ten minutes. If you can't even get out of bed, then stick your legs up in the air against a wall (which helps the blood to circulate again). Other people use a hot-water bottle – others take an everyday painkiller like paracetamol or aspirin or a specific one like Feminax. Eventually, you will get to know your cycle and can predict which days you need to take things more slowly or have the tablets handy.

A bit frightened

I'm twelve years old and in March I started my periods. Since then I've had a period every month. I seem to have one every 30 days. But recently there were only seventeen days between my periods. When I do have one it's very heavy and sometimes this dark sticky stuff comes out. Please could you tell me why my recent periods have been so irregular and also what that red sticky stuff is. Sometimes I get really scared when I'm having a period even though I think I understand all about having them. Ellen.

Answer

Periods are sometimes irregular for no special reason – especially when you've just begun having them. They'll probably settle down in time. As for what gets released from your body, it's not just blood – you're also shedding bits of 'womb lining' (unwanted since you're not going to have a baby this month!) and these bits are what you are seeing. Be assured all is well.

Pregnant 1

I'm in trouble. I've missed my last two periods. I think I'm pregnant. I've had sex with my boyfriend. I can't tell my mum 'cos she'd go mad. I have to tell someone.

Please help. PS: No, we didn't use condoms. From Pat.

Answer

Unless you act, in less than nine months' time you'll become a mum. Before this happens, it will almost certainly be obvious to the entire world that you are pregnant. So the question is *when* do you tell your parents and *how* do you break the news, not *whether* you tell them. With such a difficult message to convey it helps to have allies. Would you prefer to speak first to your doctor, teacher, aunt, best friend, best friend's mum or an organization like the Family Planning Clinic or the Brook Advisory Service (tel. 071-708 1234)? That's the best way forward and do it *now, today*. As we sit here swapping letters, the cells in your body are multiplying and the baby is growing. PS: Condoms are free from family planning clinics.

Pregnant 2

I'm writing to you because I'm having a baby. I can't have one right now because I'm only twelve years old. What am I going to do? Please help me, Phillip. My father thinks that I'm eating too many sweets and bars of chocolate. My mother also thinks that I should stop eating sweets. I don't know what to do or say. From Anon.

Answer

Look at the answer above and tell yourself to get help – you can't deal with this alone. It's a bit more serious than anything you've ever had to deal with but the quicker you tell the sooner you can stop feeling so scared and alone.

Pregnant 3

Six months ago, when my parents had gone away for the weekend, my boyfriend stayed over at my house. He asked me if I'd have sex with him. I said yes. We had sex in my parents' bed and it was nothing like I expected – it was all over in a matter of minutes. Now I think I'm pregnant. I've missed my period for a few months and just recently fluids have been coming from my breasts. I'm only thirteen years old and so cannot keep the baby. I don't know what to do and I'm thinking about suicide. Please, please help me!! Gail.

Answer

You made a mistake but it's not one you need to die for. Lots of people have done silly things like this and they've managed to enjoy good, safe, happy lives. Even if you can't keep the baby, somebody will be delighted to give your child a warm, loving home by adoption. But the facts are these: you are going to have a baby and it's almost certainly too late to think about having an abortion. You need to tell your family if you haven't done so. If you just cannot face doing this, look at the answers above and ask your doctor or the Brook Service to help.

Pregnant 4

Please help. I've just started my periods and my boyfriend (who I've been seeing for three years) asked me to have sex with him. I did because I wanted to know what it was like (it was sore). He didn't use a condom and I fell pregnant. I can't tell my mum or dad. Angela, thirteen.

Answer

See the answers above.

Pregnant 5

I'm a girl of fourteen who is in despair. A few weeks ago as I was coming home from a disco, my boyfriend invited me to his house because his parents were away. We ended up having sex. Now I'm pregnant. I told my boyfriend but he says he doesn't want anything to do with the baby. He also told me that either he goes or the unborn baby does. I love my boyfriend very much and I don't want to lose him, but if I had an abortion I would be going against my parents' beliefs – we are Catholics. Please help me. From a distressed Julie, fourteen.

Answer

Your boyfriend seems to care more for his comfort and pleasure than your future. He sounds too immature to be having sex let alone settling the fate of babies. The decision about your pregnancy is fundamentally *yours*. This is a terrible dilemma because on the one hand you're only fourteen (no age to become a mum), on the other hand you face enormous pressure from your Catholic background. You really need first-class pregnancy counselling. If you ring the Brook Advisory Service on 071-708 1234 there's still time for you to think this one through.

Pregnancy test confusion

I'm fourteen years old and my best friend is pregnant. She got a pregnancy test to see for sure. My parents were out so she tried it at my house. But my mother found it and she thinks *I'm* pregnant. I promised my friend I wouldn't tell anyone. What can I do? From a very distressed Gracie.

Answer

Then tell your mum it belongs to a friend whose identity you've promised to keep secret and swear this on your eyes, her life and the future of the human race.

And finally ... Triplet trauma

I am a fourteen-year-old girl and I am going out with a boy of sixteen. When we were at the cinema he asked me if I would go all the way with him and I did. I am now pregnant with triplets and my boyfriend has asked me to move in with him and I've said yes but haven't told my mum and dad yet and I don't know what to do. My dad's a boxer and my mum's a wrestler and they always hit me. They don't know about the babies and what I did at the cinema. Can you help? L., Glasgow.

Answer

Yes. When you're telling stories try to make them sound convincing.

5

Going All the Way

The biggest problem for teenagers in the 1990s is not to get pressured into sex before you're ready. This chapter tells you what it feels like to cope with those three awkward feelings – love, lust and fear. You can read about the biological facts and also the emotional ones – the desire to kiss, wanting to be hugged and held close, falling desperately in love, feeling ready to give yourself to someone heart and soul, suffering from guilt, dying of desire and coping with the views of your parents.

Facts of life

We are two very worried twins. We have asked our mother to explain to us the facts of life as we are thirteen. She will not tell us and neither will our friends. So please could you explain what periods and sex are?
Myra and Melanie.

Answer

I don't think there's room on this page to give you all the facts of life, although at thirteen you clearly need to know. So in addition to reading this answer, please get books from your library like *Have You Started Yet?* by Judy Green and *Sugar and Spice* by Sue Lees or *Make It Happy, Make It Safe* by Jane Mills. Sex is the act of making love, usually between a male and female, when the penis is placed inside the vagina and the bodies are moved vigorously until pleasure produces orgasm. This causes the sperm to go from the man's to the woman's body to try to fertilize one of her eggs. Sex is not legal until you are sixteen and it's not much fun unless you know what you are doing and feel ready to get involved. Having a period simply means that your body is now releasing a monthly egg and physically preparing your womb to produce a baby. Since you are too young to look after babies yet, and the egg does not meet a male sperm, it gets expelled from the body together with a bit of the womb lining. So for a few days each month, you have a 'bleed' which needs catching in a towel or tampon you can buy from a chemist's.

Age of consent

I have 3 questions to ask you to do with sex.
1. How old is the legal age of consent?
2. How old do you have to be to buy condoms?
3. How old do you have to be to buy pornographic magazines?
Please tell me because I'm very confused. Alex.

Answer

1. The age of consent for heterosexuals in the UK is 16.

But be careful on your travels – in France it's 15, Germany 14, Spain 12, Italy 14, Switzerland 16, Sweden 15, Norway 16, Luxembourg 14, Belgium 16, Hungary 14, Poland 15 but in Turkey it's 18! (For the record, the age of consent in the UK in 1880 was 12.)

2. You can buy condoms at any age. There's no law against it, you just have to find the courage.

3.So-called pornographic or 'top shelf' magazines are not supposed to be sold to minors – those under 18.

What to do 1

I am sixteen and have an eighteen-year-old boyfriend who wants to have sex with me, but I'm not sure how to do it. Does it all come naturally? When I was younger I never paid much attention to the classes we had on it, because I'm dyslexic and I didn't think anyone would want to do it with me. My parents are very protective and if they found out I'd probably be grounded for two years! If I decide to do it I will tell them I am going away with my friend for a weekend. Please help. From a sixteen-year-old, Bristol.

Answer

I'm sorry you've felt so negative about yourself and your attractions. Now you know better – people do fancy you! However, that doesn't mean you should give someone what he wants unless it's also what you want. You wouldn't travel in a foreign country without a map – why try to have sex without knowing what's involved? Sex does *not* just come naturally. We learn by reading, watching videos, talking, sharing and reassuring – then by trial and error. There's plenty of time to enjoy weeks and months of heavy petting before you go all the way. This gets you used to the whole idea – and it also shows you whether this fella is reliable and trustworthy. You should also get a leaflet on contraception from the Family Planning Association, 27-35 Mortimer Street, London W1N 7RJ.

What to do 2

There's a girl in my form who I'm going out with. My friend says that a while ago he got off with her and I'd like to as well. The problem is I'm too embarrassed to ask her and if she says yes how do I do it? Please could you tell me what to do? From a desperate twelve-year-old.

Answer

Start by holding hands. Move on to giving her a goodbye hug and kissing her cheek. When you feel closer, you may want to kiss her lips. It's all about being close. Friends brag. Don't worry about technique. If you feel intensely passionate, then you might french kiss as well – and that's called 'getting off'.

Forceful friends

I am only twelve years old and I have this problem. I have got a fourteen-year-old girlfriend and she wants to have sex with me. She didn't say it but her friends told me. Her friends are telling the truth. I am not against having sex with her but I just can't get hold of condoms. If I don't have sex with her she might pack me in. Mike.

Answer

Don't believe everything her 'friends' say. This is a classic wind-up and you should always do your own thinking about such an important move. You'll know when you're ready to handle a full sexual relationship. My advice is always to wait until you really trust the other person and could handle problems if things go wrong. For the record, condoms are free from family planning clinics and sold in chemists and supermarkets.

Peer pressure

I'm really worried. All the other people in my class have got off with someone at one time or another. I'm only thirteen and I'm not ready to have sex. If I end up pregnant I'll never forgive myself. All the people in my class make fun of me because I haven't got off with anyone. Please help. Joan.

Answer

Don't ruin your life because a bunch of mugs make fun of you. They haven't done *half* the things they boast about and getting pregnant at your age would be a disaster. When you're ready for a one-to-one, your body and mind will let you know – till then, don't let anyone push you around.

Too young to make love

I am twelve years old and I am going out with a sixteen-year-old boy. He is really nice and we get on well. We have kissed and stuff but we haven't actually got off yet. He says he will use the necessary precautions (condoms). But I am not sure if I want to go ahead with it. Please help. Deirdre.

Answer

If you are not sure you want to go ahead, then you are *not* ready, apart from the fact that he will be breaking the law if you do. It's really best to wait until you want this more than anything in the world.

He's not ready

I've recently got into a relationship with this boy. He's a year older than me which makes him seventeen. We've been going out together for quite a while now. We haven't had sexual intercourse and I'd like it very much, but he seems as though he's scared or shy. Every time we get to be alone he says things that make us come near our friends again. We're hardly ever alone. I do so much want to have sex with him but he always makes an excuse to go for a walk or something silly like that. What should I do? Anne.

Answer

I should talk to him in plain, simple terms. He may have no idea what's going on in your head (and hormones). Be sensitive as you ask your questions. Possibly he's a great deal younger than his years whereas you are the opposite.

Oral sex

Should you suck a boy off on the first date, or wait till you get to know him? Boys seem to expect a 'blow job' as soon as possible nowadays. Anon, Norwich.

Answer

Boys have always been impudent and pushy so-and-so's. They can expect the earth – you don't have to give them a grain of sand! As far as oral sex is concerned, the choice always remains yours although a first date is premature. Get to know someone's mind before you delve into their trousers.

Contraception

Lately I read in a magazine an article which said you can get pregnant if you don't contracept. I would be very grateful if you could tell me what contraception is. Thank you, Abby.

Answer

Dear Abby, contraception includes the Pill (various forms), rubber bags like the condom or the diaphragm, 'natural' methods and sterilization. What they all attempt to do is prevent a male sperm meeting up with a ripe egg inside a woman's body, although the natural method is unreliable. You can get pregnant by having sex or by heavy petting if the boy leaks any sperm near your vagina or from your fingers to your vagina. Obviously if you never have sex you won't get pregnant but if you're going to have a boyfriend, take precautions. Your family planning clinic or doctor can tell you more in confidence when the time is ripe. Remember – make sex safe before you try it. Afterwards is too late.

Sexual feelings

Me and my friend have a lot of worries between us but this is the most important worry. We would like to know what it feels like to have sex. Sorry it's so horrible but that's our worry. Is there any way you could fix it for us by helping us to feel this feeling without our parents finding out? Two worried eleven-year-old girls.

Answer

Curiosity is natural but you cannot feel 'sexy' until you

do. Very soon your bodies will go into puberty and you'll find your erotic places (breasts and clitoris) start to get very sensitive. Then you'll be able to have orgasms by masturbation – rubbing round or near your clitoris (which lies at the top of your vaginal lips). The feeling depends on your mood. An orgasm is like a spasm of joy or a burst of happiness from top to toe. Sex with a partner can feel like bliss but with a bad lover or someone you hate it's like an unpleasant operation or even a nightmare. Your question isn't horrible – everyone's interested in sex. To summarize: sex feels nice (like tingling all over and being really happy inside) when you are with someone you like and respect and you both know what you are doing and can cope should something go wrong. Sex feels nasty (like being laughed at and bruised) when you are with someone who doesn't care about you and you're too young to know how to mend your broken heart or tell them to bog off.

Definitions please

Please can you tell me what it means to lose your virginity? All my friends know but I don't. Tracey.

Answer

It just means having sexual intercourse for the first time. Virginity used to mean keeping the bit of skin across your vaginal entrance unbroken – and this is still important in some primitive cultures – but nowadays many girls stretch or break this skin by masturbating, doing PE, riding horses or using tampons.

Step-by-step instructions, please

I have thoughts about sex! I think about what you do and how. I mean, does it just happen or do you get a book of step-by-step instructions? Does the man stick his penis into the girl's vagina? When you do it do you say 'Let's go and make a baby'? I know most of the facts about how but not when. Please help. A twelve-year-old boy.

Answer

Good questions – but sex between men and women is not like digging the garden or making a model aeroplane. It's about feeling so wrapped up in someone you can't find other ways to express your delight. Yes – eventually it boils down to touching, fingering and putting a penis inside a vagina but not until you've become special best friends. The law adds and not before your sixteenth birthday. PS: sex is about more than making babies, it's about how we keep our best friendship special. Most people have sex for life but wouldn't want a baby every year.

Liked fooling around

I'm going out with this boy. Recently he invited me to his house. I accepted. When I got there his parents said they had to go out. Once they were out of sight he started to get fresh with me. To be honest, I enjoyed the first few minutes, but once I realized what I was doing I left. Now he's invited me again. I can't tell my mum but I want to go. Please help. A worried thirteen-year-old.

Answer

Your worry is there to protect you. This boy wants to have (illegal) sexual intercourse. Can you cope? I should stay on safe territory.

Doesn't want to kiss

I have a boyfriend I love very much. But I don't want to kiss him. He says he doesn't mind not kissing me, but you can tell that he does. I act very strangely when he's around. He's been out with lots of girls before but he's only my first boyfriend. Do you think I should kiss him? Samantha.

Answer

It sounds as if you have a very nice boyfriend who respects your wishes. He may want to kiss you because he likes you so much, but that doesn't mean you have to kiss him – or do anything else you feel awkward about.

Wants to kiss

I've been looking for books about french kissing and I just can't find any at all. I need the books urgently 'cause I need to work on my kissing. I know that nobody can teach you how to kiss, but I need help. I tried it on my boyfriend but it didn't work out and everyone in my school knew. It left me in tears for weeks. Please help me. Yours sincerely, Briony.

Answer

There isn't a book on french kissing – at this rate, I think I'm going to have to write one. But I did once say this on

TV: 'The tongue comes into play – usually – to french-kiss. Normally, you work up to this, rather than jump in straight away, and you tend to make sure you know the person quite well. Like everything else, it's your choice whether you do it. There's no compulsion. Only you won't want to do it twice with someone who does not clean his or her teeth properly or who has bad breath. All that happens is that as you kiss, your lips gradually part and your tongue sneaks slowly forward. If the other person opens up, then you tend to push further, and in their turn, so do they. But there's no correct method – it's just exploration.' By the way, no one knows why it's named after the French as if they were the only experts! And don't worry if this all sounds revolting – it does if you aren't interested.

Lovely long kisses

I'm thirteen and I get along very well with a boy in my form. We go around together out of school, but we've never kissed. I want to kiss him but I don't know how, and I'll look a fool when the time comes. Could you tell me how to do a basic long kiss? I've seen it on TV but I can't pick it up. Alison.

Answer

Look into his eyes and make him look into yours. Let your face show that he's special – he should feel you really want to do this. Very slowly incline your head and move towards him. This is your way of saying 'I'd like to kiss you and be kissed back – do you feel the same?' If he seems doubtful, ask in words – 'Can I kiss you?' then, if all's well, half-close your eyes (but not completely since you need to aim), pucker your mouth and gently press your lips on to his. Light brushing movements are best at first. Gradually you can apply firmer pressure and use a subtle sucking action and even open your mouth and explore further if you want. If you like it you do it some more, varying things to suit yourself.

More kisses please

My problem is that I don't know how to kiss (snog) and I don't go out with boys because of it. I know in your replies you have told other people what to do but my question is where do you put your tongue? I need to know and I can't ask my parents. Gay, aged thirteen.

Answer

Before talking about tongues, let's just say you don't have to snog in order to go out with boys. You can choose! But if you are going to start kissing soon, it's perfectly reasonable to wonder where the tongues fit in. The first few times, I suggest you keep your tongue in your mouth and kiss with the faintest pressure of lips only, slowly and gently. As you get to know each other better, you might open your mouth just a little and let your tongue flick your boyfriend's lips. Later, people get more involved and 'french' kiss, almost 'swapping' tongues inside each other's mouths. However, the important thing about kissing is not to become world champion, but to be sensitive to skin sensation. Touch your own arm with your fingernail slowly and see what I mean.

Fingering

I'm sixteen and have been going out with this boy for about eight months. I get off with him a lot. We both want to go further but I'm a bit nervous about being fingered. Please tell me what to do. Fenny.

Answer

Well, how do you like to touch yourself down there? Some women want very gentle strokes to the sides of the vaginal opening (called the vulva). Some want pressure from three or four fingers on top of their pubic mound, then down towards the clitoris. Some want delicate wet touches from one finger on the clitoris itself. Others then like the pressure to increase and speed up. Many like one or even two fingers inserted into the vagina with the end(s) curled forwards to stroke the front wall where there is a sensitive zone. Some never want to be fingered at all. You tell me.

Should I carry on?

I'm a sixteen-year-old girl. At the age of fourteen I went out with a guy I loved very much but I couldn't say it to him. Three months after my fifteenth birthday we split up. I was very upset and you could tell by my school work and moods. A few weeks later a lad came round and asked for a goodnight kiss so I gave him one. Next thing I know we are naked in each other's arms. We didn't 'do it' but we tried lots of other things. Now he keeps coming round and asking if he can have sex with me. When I say 'No' he calls me 'boring and stupid'. We do this without telling anyone. Do you think I should carry on with him? Michaela.

Answer

I can't see a lot of point in 'carrying on' with someone who insults you. Especially when you already feel bad about a broken relationship. Another lousy experience won't help. Sure, you're curious about sex and touching feels wonderful. But you'd do yourself a big favour by waiting till your heart is mended and you have someone worthwhile in your arms.

Bullied into bed

I'm fourteen years old and have a boyfriend aged sixteen. A few months back he asked me to go to bed with him. The answer was no. Until recently he's been neglecting me, but the other day he asked me to think again about going to bed with him. I can't decide what to say, for I know that if I say no he will dump me, and if I say yes the result could be fatal. From a worried fourteen-year-old. Davida.

Answer

The answer's still no because you're under-age and he's unreliable. The all-time worst reason to make love is because you're afraid of being dumped. I'm afraid it means the relationship is rotten and the experience is likely to be lousy.

Travellers' tales

My friend and I've got mixed up with some travellers. They're really nice and treat us well. We love them. They are both eighteen and we are both fifteen. We often go on a spin in one of their cars and have a laugh – nothing serious. The problem is they have asked us to have sex with them. We haven't told them our answer yet. We don't know what to do. We're both virgins and really want to have sex with them. We're afraid to say no in case we might lose them. What shall we do? Sharon.

Answer

The worst reason for sleeping with someone is in case you lose them. It means they don't care about the rest of you. When they've had their fun, you're still likely to lose them. I suggest you wait until you meet someone who wants more than a passing fling in a car.

Safe sex

I met the girl of my dreams at a disco last week and we were snogging from about ten till two in the morning. But when I asked her back to my place she gave me loads of questions about Aids and HIV and I didn't have any answers. I don't really know what safe sex is. Brian, seventeen.

Answer

I'm glad you both asked. Safer sex means having fewer partners, using barrier protection like a condom and avoiding high-risk people and practices. However, for a fuller story listen to my new audio-tape *Phillip Hodson's Guide to Sex and Relationships* which you can get from CSA, 101 Chamberlayne Road, London NW10 3ND, £8 (two cassettes) inc p & p.

Not ready for sex

I'm fifteen years old and being pressured into sex by my eighteen-year-old boyfriend. I love him a lot and don't want to hurt his feelings by pushing him away – but how can I tell him every night when we kiss in privacy and he tries to undress me that he has to wait another night? I really want sex but don't think I can face it yet because I've only been having my period for two months. I'm frightened because I don't want to face sex but I don't want to face losing him. What can I do? Gabriella.

Answer

This is a tough situation but you're not yet ready for intercourse. You don't make love because someone else piles on the pressure, nor is the sex much good. Tell him you love him and love kissing him but you'll decide when you want to take more clothes off. Is there a teacher or school nurse you can discuss this with?

Risky sex

I'm fifteen years old and I really need to go on the contraceptive pill urgently. When I go out to night clubs I meet fellas and sometimes end up having sex with them. I do ask them to wear condoms but very often they don't want to. I'm usually too aroused to argue. I don't want you to get the wrong idea about them making me have sex because they don't. Please help. Don't say talk to your mum, she'll understand, because I don't have that sort of relationship with her. Kathy.

Answer

It's crazy for you to have such risky sex. I bet your partners don't even know you're under-age, especially when you're in make-up. Please contact your nearest Brook Advisory centre and make the effort to go for contraceptive counselling. (The Brook Advisory Service's central office telephone number is 071-708 1234; there is also a 24-hour automated helpline on 071-410 0420.) Whatever boys want, you should be protected.

Going All the Way

Girlfriend is not ready for sex

I am eighteen. My girlfriend is fifteen. We are both
virgins. I want to have sex. My girlfriend says no. But if
you don't make it with your partner how can you show
love? We agreed nothing should happen till we both
wanted it. But we've been together for four months and
I'm ready now. Tom.

Answer

But she is not, and the three-year difference in your
ages may well be proving decisive. I suspect you are
both 'virginity anxious' – you to lose it, she to keep it.
You both seem concerned about 'proofs' of love. You
think love means saying yes. She thinks love means not
bothering her, plus she protects herself with the deal
you both agreed. In fact, love is not about power or
making people do things. That's why your relationship
is not yet good enough to be sexual. So it's not your
wishes that can be faulted, but your understanding. If
you wish to have sex today, now, at this minute, then it
cannot be with her. You must move on. But if you
would like to know how to express love and to see what
sexual reward it can ultimately bring, then tell her you
can see her point of view, explain your anxiety, describe
your frustration and show her in words, kisses, sighs
and looks how much you continue to care about her. Do
this for long enough and she will feel she can trust you
all the way.

We all make mistakes

This boy talked me into letting him have sex when I
didn't want to and next day his friend came and tried to

do the same, saying as I'd done it for one, I'd do it for the other. I was a bit drunk then, and I don't know how I'll ever face my friends again. Maya.

Answer

Let she that is without sin cast the first stone ... We are all prone to make mistakes (thank goodness, because otherwise we'd never learn a thing). Tell yourself, and others if necessary, that this was an error of judgement on your part. For just a minute, you believed this young man was worth having.

The Aids dilemma

I'm nineteen, have been in my first sexual relationship for two years but can now see it's not going to last, certainly not for a lifetime. How do I start again, knowing I might run the risk of contracting Aids? Nikki.

Answer

As more heterosexuals acquire HIV, this is going to be one of the big dilemmas over the next fifteen years. Your bitter choice (which the older generation uniformly feels sad and guilty about, though that's small consolation) is between celibacy on the one hand, and trying to minimize the risks on the other. If sex is to remain part of your life, then you have to pick lovers carefully, get to know their background before exploring their bodies, consider the pros and cons of HIV-testing, use condoms and avoid high-risk behaviour (including unguarded sex with extra partners). In the early days of a relationship, it is prudent to avoid penetration, preferring mutual masturbation, unless and until you are sure the man is going to become a regular boyfriend. This is in his interest every bit as much as yours. If he complains, quote this slogan: 'They used to say masturbation could kill you. Now they say it could save your life.'

Misunderstandings

I love girls, I just can't help myself. But the girls always seem to think the words 'I love you' imply some kind of exclusive commitment. I'm always in trouble because just after orgasm I tell them I love them. Nicholas.

Answer

The need to express love after intercourse is often the need to say how wonderful and grateful you feel, or how much you like sex itself. Why not re-phrase your appreciation along such lines as 'That was lovely' or 'You're marvellous' or 'I'm so happy'? Then your partner could neither take offence nor feel misled.

6

Same-Sex Worries

Not everyone is going to grow up 'straight' – about 2–5 per cent of the population will become homosexual. The difficulty during teenage is how to label your feelings. It's quite normal at fifteen to fall in fascination with someone of your own sex even though you may eventually grow up to be heterosexual. The important thing is to keep an open mind and to offer love, respect and consideration to all your friends.

Confused feelings

I'm fourteen years old and have a problem. I belong to a swimming club in Hampshire. Before I went there I thought I was gay. Now I'm at the club I've met this really good-looking girl called S—. She is the woman of my dreams, but I am not sure whether I am still gay. Please could you give me advice? Peter.

Answer

The answer is: some people know for a fact they're gay at fourteen and never look at the opposite sex. A lot of straight people have crushes on their own sex at around fourteen but remain straight. Anyone like you who is *unsure* at fourteen could well be heterosexual. So it's really not very helpful to label yourself. Just live your life.

Hands off please!

My friend and I have another friend who's a bit mad with other girls and gets carried away. When we're round at her house she tries to throw you on her bed and lie on top of you and things like that. She also tries to touch you in the places you don't want her to. We'd like to tell her to get off and go away, but she's very sensitive and we don't want her to break up with us. Please help. From Elaine and Kathie.

Answer

Always say *no* to objectionable behaviour. Tell her you still like her but can she please stop being 'insensitive' to your feelings and keep her hands to herself? Come on, there's two of you – get stroppy.

Too embarrassed to go to school

I have a problem. I am a girl and I fancy a girl at school and once I kissed her. She told all her friends. Now I am so embarrassed. It has got to the point where I bunk off school. Whatever shall I do? Marjorie.

Answer

Well, stop bunking off school because that means you really are ashamed of yourself. You can't help feeling this way and it's not so unusual to get attached to close friends, so don't give yourself grief. The real embarrassment is the mob. They can't deal with their reaction. So why do you help them? Just walk past. If you ignore it, in the end they'll go and pick on someone else. Just be yourself.

Frightened of friend

Please help me. I have got this friend (male) who keeps touching me where he should not. I am sure he is gay and I try keeping away from him but he follows me everywhere and he once asked me around to his house because his parents were out. I don't know what to do now. Callum.

Answer

You own your body and only you can give permission for someone to touch it. So when this rule gets broken, you must speak up – 'Don't touch me like that, I don't like it.' If the problem continues, tell someone who can intervene. You should never keep a secret that screws you up.

Rumours caused problems

I am fourteen years old and go to an all-girls' school. Two years ago there were rumours going around because I told a so-called friend that I loved this other girl. Because of this stupidity, I wasn't the only one who suffered. The girl herself was teased rotten and she got really upset. She still talked to me even though we were both called lesbians. However, I can't bring myself to get close to her now because of the rumours. I haven't spoken to her for two years though I'd love to be her best friend, but not more. Gemma.

Answer

One of the biggest problems in school is vicious teasing. 'Friends' as well as 'enemies' do it to get power over you. You have to decide whether to let them. Tell yourself the real inadequacy is theirs. Strong people wouldn't bother. Tell yourself to 'let it wash over you'. And tell yourself they are *not* going to win. You can be friends with anyone, or 'love' them, without being sexually implicated.

Worried about friend

We're two worried friends aged thirteen. We suspect that our other friend prefers women to men. We first thought this when she started staring at us. Now she's begun coming up and putting her arm round us and she's begun to stroke our hair and walking close to us. She doesn't do this to her other friends and we don't want to confront her in case we're wrong. What shall we do? Anons.

Answer

Just say 'Stop it!' You don't have to give a reason. Part of growing up is needing to be in charge of your own body – even with friends. She's probably desperate for attention and a little pushy.

Bosomy pal

I have a friend and when we go swimming and I'm getting changed, she touches my breasts. I feel really embarrassed and I'm beginning to hate her. Please help. I don't know where else to turn. Daniela.

Answer

Look her straight in the eye, speak slowly and clearly, and tell her to knock it off.

Attracted to same-sex teachers

I'm a fifteen-year-old girl and last year I thought I was a lesbian because I felt very strongly for one of my teachers. This feeling wouldn't go away and I ended up avoiding this teacher completely. Then I read in a magazine that this usually happens to all teenagers at some time. So I dismissed it. But now I have started to like another teacher (also female) and I'm completely obsessed with her and find myself constantly trying to attract her attention. I've started to daydream about what it would be like if I was her lover. Am I a lesbian? Tracey.

Answer

Crushes on teachers don't provide an answer because nearly everyone gets them. You may simply want emotional attention, and from *more* than one teacher. The sensible thing is to make as many good friends as you can regardless of age or sex.

Gay classmate

A couple of days ago a fourteen-year-old boy in our class admitted he was gay and now it has gone all round the school. People are saying they don't want to get undressed for games with him in the same changing room. He has even told the teachers he is gay but I don't think they are doing anything about it. What should we do? Barry.

Answer

He's no more of a threat than he was a week ago, so carry on treating him like a human being. Have a private chat with the games teacher if you want to but the class should be safe from one bloke!

Crush on teacher

I'm in the fifth year and I seem to have an obsession about a teacher. I'm a female and so is the teacher. She's a caring person and I just can't get her out of my mind. She's like a 'mentor'. Whenever I see her my heart misses a beat. I think about her 24 hours a day and dream she's my mother. I get very depressed if I don't see her. Why have I an attraction for her? Is this normal? I was physically and mentally abused when I was younger. Should I tell her about this and about how I feel, or suffer in silence? I need someone I can talk to, but I don't know who. Donna.

Answer

When you're a teenager, it's perfectly normal to have a crush on a teacher or doctor or friend's parent. This has nothing to do with being sexually abused as a youngster since it happens to thousands of kids who've had happy childhoods. Your word 'mentor' ('wise counsellor') is right since you're modelling yourself on someone you admire. Trying to decide what sort of adult to be is difficult. You don't want to be exactly like mum and dad or you can't feel special. Yet you need a bit of guidance and in your heart of hearts you feel drawn to a person who seems sympathetic and supportive. Where your personal background may make a difference is in the *intensity* of these feelings. Perhaps you've always felt let down by the grown-ups? I know you've experienced great bouts of insecurity. As a result, your crush may seem overwhelming but try not to worry. It's good to enjoy such strong natural emotion. By all means speak to this teacher. I think you could avoid a lot of problems now and in the future by discussing your past. But proceed carefully. Just because you 'worship' someone from afar doesn't mean they feel the same way about you. This means asking permission to speak about your difficulties – 'I like you, can I talk to you – will you listen to me?' – before you go further. But don't declare undying, passionate love because that will be misinterpreted. Perhaps you two could become friends?

Obsession

I have this really big crush on a boy in my class. I'm fifteen and he's sixteen. I know that he doesn't feel the same, but he knows that I like him. The problem is that this crush is becoming an obsession. I can never stop thinking about him. I'd do anything for him (and I do). I give him money, buy his lunch, I even quit my paper round to let him have it. I think that now he's playing on that and taking me for granted. To top it all off I am also a boy, and the whole school is calling me things (but not him) all the time. Please help as I'm really confused. Am I gay or is it just a phase?

Answer

I don't think the word 'gay' is helpful to you because your feelings don't seem to be sexual. There are some people who've known they are gay from the age of ten. But equally, every teenager can experience strong same-sex attachments, even loving passions, and yet go on to become totally 'straight'. So the answer to your question is 'probably not gay'. A better way to describe your feelings is 'obsessive hero worship'. Again, many teenagers strongly admire the 'leaders' in their group or class. This is a way of moving beyond the family and its values by modelling your behaviour on such people, copying their mannerisms and gestures, language and habits. At present, you're getting the balance all wrong. Far from adding this boy's better qualities to your own, it seems you just want to be him, as if you didn't like yourself at all! As a result, you are trying to buy his favours with disastrous consequences. Remember that money can't buy you love. He's not worth your regard if he needs to be bribed. Work on your confidence, in particular why you don't feel so good about yourself. When did this start? If someone's criticized you so much that you feel 'inferior' it's time to fight back. Try to establish some additional friendships on an equal footing. Practise your confidence skills – talking, questioning, generally making your voice heard. When people tease you don't give them the pleasure of getting annoyed – smile and move on.

How to tell 1

My mother keeps asking when I'm going to get a boyfriend (I'm eighteen) and I keep funking telling her. How do you tell your mother you are gay?

Answer

The answer depends on your mother. If you're convinced she's the sort of person who'd say 'Do not darken my door again', you may never want to tell her out of sensible self-interest. If your mum is reasonably open, you may decide to go ahead but choosing time, place and circumstance carefully. For instance, ensure when you talk she is neither tired, angry, busy nor hungry. Even then, pick your words. Instead of bleakly announcing, 'I am a lesbian', say 'I've fallen in love with a friend who happens to be a woman.' For all the sad stories of children being disowned, the majority of parents are eventually supportive. One heartening tale comes from a family where the mother replied, 'As a matter of fact, there have been times when I thought I was gay too.'

How to tell 2

The other day my dad came into my room (I am eighteen) and said, 'Have you anything to tell me?' I replied No. He repeated the question, then said, 'Are you one of them?' When I admitted I was gay, he said 'Where did we go wrong?' and 'Why are you doing this to us?' I still don't know what to tell him.

Answer

You will probably have to tell your father that he has

done absolutely nothing 'wrong'. Nor are you 'doing this to them'. You simply are homosexual. They may not like it, but your sexual identity is neither defiance nor disaster. It simply closes down some options, which may make them feel sad, while opening up others. There is often no obvious 'cause' of a sexual orientation, gay or straight. It's more like a lifetime's evolution of tastes for which there is no scientific accounting. Why do some parents like comedy on TV, old dance-band music, root beer and heavily-embossed wallpaper? These questions are more trivial but the answers are equally hard to find. Be patient, as your parents come to terms with this.

Lesbian concerns

We have got a very worrying problem. Our friend keeps on touching us in certain places and she tries to squeeze our breasts. After school she pushes us into a corner and tells us to pull down our pants. She also tries to kiss us. We are sure she is a lesbian. Please tell us what to do. Gwen and Tina.

Answer

Well, she's obviously a nuisance – you make her sound like a randy puppy. If she won't behave herself, I should threaten to end the friendship once and for all.

Gay friend

I have a friend who everyone thinks is gay. Recently they've started accusing me of being gay, too. And what's worse, they are saying we are doing things together. I can't ignore them and I dread to think what my parents would say if they heard. I've even considered telling everyone that I *am* gay just to get them off my back. From Martin.

Answer

I don't think that would help – they'd probably tease you even more. You can't stop people making suggestions so it's best to shrug these off. You know who you are and what you have or haven't done.

Confused feelings 1

I'm eleven years old and my feelings are changing. I think I may be gay because I really like a boy in my class at school. I kissed him on the lips and we touched each other on our private parts. Could we get Aids from this? From Anon.

Answer

No, because I'd bet you're both virgins and because kissing and touching are thought to be 'safe' sexual practices.

Confused feelings 2

Please help. I am a homosexual and I've known about this since the age of twelve. I'm now fourteen. I have made five scrapbooks full to the brim with pictures of topless men. I have a male cousin who is nine, and whenever we meet we go to bed with each other, imagining that we are husband and wife. Is this against the law? I started puberty when I was twelve. I now wank almost every night. Am I going to turn sterile? The thing that I cannot understand is that I go all shy when I meet girls. I fantasize about having sex with them. But I do this with men as well. Am I bisexual? Of course I talk freely at school about girls. Nobody knows about me being supposedly gay. Please help. Anthony.

Answer

You've got more than your fair share of confusions. Yes, it's technically illegal for you to go to bed with another male because the age of consent in this country for private, gay sex is 21. No, wanking won't make you sterile, just orgasmic. Yes, you seem to have bisexual fantasies – maybe you've turned to boys partly because you are so shy in the presence of girls? If so, it would be silly to miss out on experience with females when shyness can so easily be overcome – just write to me for a shyness leaflet.

How to come out

I have a very big problem. I am gay. My family *do* know but I do not know how to tell my friends. I've a boyfriend and his parents don't know that he is gay. Please can you tell me how to tell my friends about me, or even if I should? I think that some of them must know as I have never had a girlfriend, and I always walk around with boys. I'm seventeen years old. From very upset and puzzled.

Answer

If you tell people, do it gradually and give them time to react. Maybe it'll be a shock even if they have suspected the truth. Only do it if you feel it will really help YOU – you're not doing it to improve others!

Excited by another girl

I am madly in love with a girl in my class. Every time I

brush past her I feel an electric sensation, like I have won something. I don't want to be a lesbian, but I really do love her. Please help as I don't know what to do. Angie.

Answer

Why not enjoy this great feeling rather than get into a panic? Nobody can say it is wrong to love another person. Enjoy the friendship and ignore silly labels.

Kissing boys

My problem is I invited a friend round for tea last week. My family were at work and my friend and I went to my bedroom to listen to some tapes. Suddenly my friend kissed me. I just let him do it. The strange thing is that I enjoyed it. Since then we have been seeing each other every day and kissed often. Does this mean we're gay? Derek.

Answer

It's possible. Perhaps you two should talk about it and find out what you both think.

Sex games

The crowd of boys I go around with meets at a nearby park. We play sex games like feeling each other's penises and masturbating together. I enjoy this. Does this mean I'm gay? Paul.

Answer

Not as such – it means you're very curious about sex. Loads of guys do things like this at fourteen or fifteen and yet never show any sexual interest in men later on.

Some of course do.

Jealous of friend

I'm a thirteen-year-old boy. I fancy this other boy in my class. We've been best friends since infant school. He's been going out with a girl for about one year now. Every time I see them together I think of killing myself. A worried teenager.

Answer

A better idea would be to realize that you're jealous. If you've been friends for that long of course it hurts when this guy turns to someone new. Remind him to stay friends with you despite his other interests.

7

Bad Touching

This chapter looks at abuse – sexual, violent and verbal. We have an advantage nowadays that the subject can be discussed – when I grew up nobody would talk about it. There is one golden rule to remember: your body belongs to you and nobody else, not even your parents. If anyone touches you in a way which feels shameful or wrong, you should always speak up – tell, tell and tell again. Remember, there's nothing you can do to CAUSE abuse – the grown-ups who do it are ALWAYS at fault, so never accept the blame.

Fear of stepdad

I am thirteen years old. Four months ago my stepdad came into my room. He started talking to me in a way I've never heard him speak before. He asked me to undress in front of him. I said no and told him to get out. Then a few weeks later he came into my room and told me he would give me money if I'd take off my top in front of him. I refused. Lately, when he thinks I'm asleep, I can see him spying through the crack in my door. I can't tell my mum because she has so many problems of her own. I've told my best friend and she suggested I write and tell you. Please help me. Anon.

Answer

I understand how bad you must be feeling about this, especially since it's difficult to talk to mum when she's under stress. However, so far you've done all the right things, especially saying no to your creepy stepdad as loudly and firmly as you can. You've also talked to your best friend and me – well done. The way forward is *always* to tell and complain. You have the right to scream *No* because none of this is your fault. This man has no business touching or ogling your body whatever his relationship with your mum. The problem is entirely and completely his. He probably needs expert treatment but even this is not *your* responsibility to sort out. You don't owe him a thing. Your job is to look after you. You may not be able to do this alone and I hope you get the message that other people are there to help you. Call the NSPCC Child Protection Line at once. The freephone number is 0800 800 500. They will talk through all the options *before* you make any further move and can also supply helpful leaflets. You don't have to make any official complaint until you want to. Try to tell your mum. She probably needs to find out sooner rather than later and she may feel a lot worse if it's later. If you decide a social worker should investigate officially don't imagine your family is going to be destroyed. In most cases, nobody is taken into care or leaves home. The sole goal is to keep you safe. Sexual abuse doesn't just happen in 'freak' families so don't think things will never get right. If you take the help on offer, you'll come through without any further damage.

Fear of grandpa

Please help me – whenever I go up to my gran's (when my parents aren't there), my grandpa comes into my room and does things. I have to go up there again in December and am very worried about it. I don't want to upset my mum. Glenda.

Answer

If any grown-up frightens you or tries to touch you in a way which makes you feel unsafe *always tell on them*. I know this can be difficult. But what they are doing is wrong and you need help against them because they are bigger. Remember it is *never* your fault if an older person picks on you like this. If you can't tell your mum straight away, get someone else to help you find the confidence. Is there a teacher at school who seems friendly and safe? Then tell them. You have to make sure you do not get hurt again in December. If the first grown-up you tell doesn't believe you, keep telling until someone does. It might not be easy, but even though something has already happened, try to tell now. If anyone older than you, even someone you know, ever tries to kiss or touch you in a way you don't like or that confuses you, or which they say is supposed to be a secret, say NO in a very loud voice. Wherever you are, it is all right to yell if someone is trying to hurt you. Practise yelling as loud as you can in a big deep voice by taking a deep breath and letting the yell come from your stomach, not just from your throat. If you get really stuck, these are the places you can telephone: 1. Childline is free – just dial 0800 1111; 2. The National

Society for the Prevention of Cruelty to Children can be reached day or night on their Child Protection Helpline, freephone 0800 800 500; 3. The Samaritans are also there 24 hours a day (see your local telephone book); 4. Or you can call Kidscape on 071-730 3300.

Fear of uncle

Please help me. Whenever I go to my uncle's and auntie's (when my parents aren't there), my uncle comes into my room at night without my auntie knowing and tries to feel me and french kiss me. I am going up there soon and I am very scared. I need your help. I dare not tell my family or friends as they all think he's great. I am only twelve years old and don't like what's happening. Cyan.

Answer

But they won't think he's so great once you speak up. It may take a little time to convince them and you need to choose very carefully who you tell first. But do it – don't put up with the pain and hurt of this awful secret for a moment longer.

Scared to talk about it

Please could you help me? I don't want to talk to anybody so please don't tell me to spill the beans. I feel if certain people find out my life won't be worth living. Could you please give me a way of coping by myself? When I was ten a family friend used to come around to our home. He would use the excuse of wanting to read me a bedtime story, and then after the story he would get on top of me. Afterwards, he would go home to his wife and two grown-up children as if nothing had happened. I am now fifteen and I can't relax around males, no matter if it is a friend, relative, teacher or even my father. How can I tell myself it is all right and everybody is not like that man? How can I trust the male sex again? Please help. You are my last hope of becoming normal. Gracie.

Answer

You have to test people and that means talking to them. It's because you can't speak of these bad times you can never find out what other males are like. For instance, most boys would be upset and shocked to hear you've been attacked like this. You would be able to read their concern in their faces. But if you never tell them anything, then you just go on imagining the worst about the entire sex. It's also by starting to trust in very small ways that gradually you gain new confidence and can even think of men as friends again.

Teacher trouble

We have just moved up to secondary school and we are very worried about our French teacher. He keeps playing with our hair when we work, and when we sing songs he tries to look down our tops. He gives us the creeps. What can we do? From two worried twelve-year-old girls, Shirley and Carol.

Answer

Say in a very strong voice, 'Leave my hair alone, please.' If this doesn't work, tell your parents at once. They can certainly deal with the school.

Headteacher trouble

I'm a fourteen-year-old boy and have a really big problem. One day I got sent to the headmaster's office because I was talking. He chatted for a while then suddenly asked me if I had tried sex before. I said No. So he stroked my face and started getting really sick. I tried to run out but he blocked the door so I got out by the window. I can't tell anyone about this and don't know what to do.

Answer

Again, you have to tell. This man is supposed to be looking after you not assaulting you. Chances are if it's happened to you it's also happened to others, who may choose to speak up. If you don't tell, it's more likely to happen to more boys in future. Follow the advice given in the first two answers in this chapter.

Boy at school

I'm twelve and one of the boys at my school has been sexually abusing his sister. I can't stop him but I did tell my mum to ring the school and report it. Hopefully it will stop. It must be a dreadful experience for his sister. From Ann.

Answer

Talk to your mum again to see what happened. You could also ask the girl how she's getting on.

Boyfriend pressure

I've just started my periods and my boyfriend is

pressurizing me to go to bed with him. I'm thirteen and he's eighteen. If I refuse he hits me and he said he'd tell everyone that we did it anyway. Please help. I'm very scared. Jennifer.

Answer

Get him into trouble by complaining first to your parents and if possible to the police. No one should be abused and bullied into having sex – he's a potential rapist.

Naked neighbour

Every night when I go to bed, I look out the window and see the boy across the road looking at me. When he sees me he quickly strips off his clothes and stands naked in the window. He always covers his face. What shall I do? I daren't tell my parents and I certainly don't want to tell his. Eleanor.

Answer

Stop looking – he'll soon give up without an audience.

Sister's boyfriend

I'm fourteen and my big sister and her boyfriend have been going out for about five years and they are now engaged. When they come to our house or I go to theirs, he starts touching me where he should not. Once he opened up my shirt and started touching me. I got frightened and angry but I couldn't get away. When I'm wearing a T-shirt he always tries to put his hand up it. I used to like it when they visited, but now I just get scared and afraid. Please help me. Debra.

Answer

Tell your mum and ask her to sort this out. Perhaps she could have a word with him alone, as some kind of final warning. You shouldn't have to cope with your sister's randy boyfriend. Better to deal with it now before he's officially joined the family.

Boyfriend's brother

Please help me. My boyfriend invites me over to his house every Wednesday when his mum and dad are out. My boyfriend is twelve and goes to football club at 6 p.m. He says just to watch TV and he's back in an hour. The problem is his brother who is thirteen. He threatens me by saying 'I want you to frenchie me otherwise I'll beat you up.' Since there's no one there I can't stop him. But the last time it was all too much and he said that unless I took all my clothes off and got on the floor with him he'd tell my boyfriend that I wanted to have it off with him, so again I obeyed. I've tried asking my boyfriend if I can come round when he's with me all the time, but he just asks why and I end up lying. I've even tried talking to his brother, but no luck. I've tried ringing Childline but my sister is always with me and I don't want her to know. What shall I do? From Gina, aged twelve.

Answer

Have some confidence that people will believe you and not the lies of others. You can't let boys push you around like this. Meet your boyfriend when he gets back from football. If his brother tries it on again tell on him at once.

Worried sister

I have a problem. I'm thirteen and my brother is three. My brother keeps on talking about sex, saying let's stick willies and diddies together. I don't know if I should tell my mum. Somebody has told him, but who? Please help me. Sara.

Answer

Sara, I don't think this means your brother has had a nasty experience though it's good to know you're looking out for him. Young boys of his age naturally talk about their willies. By all means have a reassuring chat with your mum but it's probably all perfectly innocent.

Abusive boyfriend

My boyfriend slapped me round the face with a shoe and I started bleeding. I went to the hospital. Then one night he came around to my house. My mum and dad were out. My sister let him in and he came upstairs. He closed the door and started to undress me. Please can you help me as I think I'm pregnant. Susie, fourteen.

Answer

You've been attacked and abused and need help fast. If you can't bear to tell your parents yet, contact the Brook Advisory Service on 071-708 1234 who can offer you confidential pregnancy advice. They can also talk to you about dealing with your family's reaction to this problem.

Over-friendly cousin

I'm a thirteen-year-old girl who's very worried about Boxing Day. Every year my older cousin who's seventeen comes to visit me and my family. At night he comes into my bedroom to play the computer. But for the past two years he asks me many questions about growing up, and also asks me if I want him to show me how to have a snog. I've told my parents but they don't believe me. He's coming to visit this Boxing Day and I don't know what to do. Cheryl.

Answer

I'm sure your parents believe you. The problem is that they don't think it's very serious. I disagree, because you're upset. If your cousin steps out of line again, tell them calmly that he's badgering you and they have to put a stop to it. At the very least, put the computer in another room on Boxing Day.

Bad feelings

I'm fourteen years old and I've done something dreadfully wrong. Recently I let a seventeen-year-old boy put his fingers in me. He asked me if I would have sex but I said no. After he left I found I had blood all over me. I ran into the bathroom and cried, scrubbing myself raw. Now I feel dirty, slaggish and can't face myself or bear to look at my body. I don't even think I can tell anyone but you. All I do now is cry when I am alone. Last year my stepdad sexually assaulted me and this recent incident brings back bad memories and I have nightmares. My stepfather is gone but the boy and memories are still there. From Alice.

Answer

Your stepdad treated you like dirt but that doesn't change you – you're clean through and through. I understand why this bad memory returns to haunt you, and you blame yourself, especially when you have sexy thoughts today. But please believe me when I say none of this is your fault. You need to confide in someone soon who can understand what's happened. Try to tell a teacher or counsellor at school.

Father going too far

I'm writing to you because I have this problem. My dad hits and touches me. I'm thirteen and have a baby brother who'll be one soon. Since mum left in January he hits me when he comes home from work. Normally it's because I haven't bathed the baby or something petty. My brother has a nanny looking after him until I get home from school, then I take over. Dad doesn't hit him. Last week he undid my bra and he touched me. As there wasn't anyone there he pulled and twisted my nipples. Please help me as I'm really scared. Dora.

Answer

Dora, you have to get away from this situation as soon as possible. Right now, your dad is not fit to be in charge of two children. Please call the NSPCC Child Protection Helpline on (freephone) 0800 800 500.

Raped by stepdad

I have a problem and I don't know how to tell my mum. My stepdad raped me when my mum was at work. I can't tell my mum because she's so in love with him. If I tell my mum, that will break them up. I don't want that to happen. From a ten-year-old girl.

Answer

Your facts are wrong. *You* matter as much as anyone else and if it's a choice between upsetting mum and keeping quiet, you have to tell your mum. Just think – right now she imagines this is a great guy, and she's *wrong*. It would really be best for her to know what a bad thing he has done to you. Please tell.

Abused by baby-sitter

I am thirteen years old and I have a problem. One day my mum and her boyfriend went out and left a baby-sitter. He was around seventeen years old. We were watching TV until around 11 o'clock and then he said, 'Bed time.' I didn't like it when he said that. I went up to my room and five minutes later he came to my door. He got hold of me and stripped me and touched me in places no one does. I'm so afraid to tell my mum. What should I do? Jean.

Answer

Always tell your mum – I know it's difficult to know how to start but adults can cope if you tell them slowly, and repeat the important bits. This guy needs stopping now.

Afraid of the men making passes

I am big for my age and my breasts are very big. I'm thirteen years old but I look about twenty. Men keep making passes at me. It really scares me when this happens. I'm always pretending that I'm ill to avoid going out. The other day a man asked me to go to bed with him. I refused and ran home. Please help. Celina, Shropshire.

Answer

Don't hide. If thoughtless men say these things, tell them to 'Bog off!' in a very loud voice.

8

Families and Friends

We all rely on our families but we all suffer from them too. When it comes to sex and adolescence, few parents are totally understanding – they've forgotten what it was like to be young, or they don't realize how far 'times have changed'. Current teenagers not only have to cope with traditional family rules and rows about things like sex and staying up late. They also have to deal with parents divorcing or having affairs under their very noses. One difficulty is standard – can you talk to mum and dad about what's really bothering you? At times you want to desperately – at other times wouldn't dream of it.

Pushy date

I'm thirteen years old and extremely mature for my age. Down my road there's a boy who's sixteen and he often looks at me. The other day he asked me out to the cinema and I said yes. During the film he asked me if I wanted to get off with him? I didn't answer. I went out of the cinema and he followed me back to my house. My parents were not in. He came in and shut the door. When I went upstairs to my room, he followed me. He pushed the door open and we fell on the bed. My parents walked in and he ran out of the door. My parents grounded me and told me never to see him again. I know this sounds stupid but I still fancy him. What shall I do? Gill.

Answer

I should be careful. If you see him again you are bound to get into trouble with your parents. And with a boy this pushy, you are likely to get into trouble anyway – he doesn't seem very bothered about your needs.

Banned from girlfriend

I've got a really big problem. I've got a girlfriend who I really love and have known all my life. We are writing letters to each other now because when I went round to her house I threw a rugby ball through the window. Now her mum won't let her see me because she says I'm naughty. What shall I do? From Guy, thirteen, desperate.

Answer

Get some flowers together (ask your parents if you can buy some or pick some) and take them round to your girlfriend's mum. Say you're really sorry about the window and can you see your friend again because you'll never ever bring a rugby ball within two miles of her house. By the way – people do get over being angry.

Nudity at friend's house

I'm a fifteen-year-old girl who has just moved to a new area. I've made a great friend at my new school. The problem is she and her family are very open. When she invited me to her house for tea the other day, we were in her bedroom listening to records when her father came in. He said hello and asked my friend to run him a bath while he got undressed. After his bath, he just walked into my friend's bedroom drying his hair with a towel but otherwise stark naked. He asked my friend to find the hair-drier and she did. Then they sat chatting away as if it were normal. When he left, she simply asked if I thought her dad was still attractive for his age. Do you think this is wrong? Maureen.

Answer

His behaviour made you feel uncomfortable. He's showing-off or insensitive. Don't get me wrong. The human body is wonderful and nudism in the right place can be great fun. But the right place is not his daughter's bedroom – nor do you 'flash' at your daughter's friends. In future, I'd play records at *your* house.

Father's affair

I'm a fifteen-year-old boy and I'm so depressed because just recently I discovered that my father was having an affair with another woman. Three days ago, my mother and older brother went out to the shops and I saw him in the lounge kissing this woman. I can't talk to anyone and I'm the only one who knows. I thought about telling my godmother but it's just finding the guts to speak.

Answer

It always feels terrible when the adults break the rules. But you don't even know how serious this kissing may prove, and many marriages do survive affairs. To ease the pressure, tell your godmother you think your parents aren't getting on very well and you're having nightmares about a possible divorce. Can she (discreetly) find out what's happening?

Caught dad kissing another woman

On Saturday nights our mum goes out with the girls and my dad stays in. Our dad tells us to go to bed at eight sharp. I'm twelve and my sister is nine. One night I went downstairs to tell my dad that my sister felt sick, but when I walked in I caught my dad snogging another woman. He shouted, 'Get back to bed.' I ran upstairs crying. I told my sister about it, but in the morning we didn't know whether to tell our mum or not. What should we do?

Answer

I don't think you should tell your mum because you haven't got all the facts. Some kisses are silly; some don't matter. There could be a terrible misunderstanding. But you do need a private chat with someone – try an aunt or teacher – to get it off your chest.

Lying to parents

I'm twelve years old and I go out with a fourteen-year-old. The only problem is my parents. They won't let me go out with boys till I'm sixteen. I don't think this is right. My boyfriend asks me if I want to go somewhere so I lie to my mum and say I'm going to a friend's. If my parents found out I had a boyfriend they would ground me for months. It's not fair. All my friends have boyfriends and their parents are pleased!!! What can I do? From a sad, annoyed Philippa.

Answer

Try not to think too badly of your parents – they're being protective. Lying makes you feel bad so try to see your friend when you are in a group. If over the next year you show your family you haven't become a badly-behaved monster with three heads, they'll have to come round.

Worried about the pill

I recently found out my mum was on the pill. Nobody told me – I just found them in the cupboard. Please, please tell me what it means and what is the reason for taking them? Andrew.

Answer

Relax. It just means your mum is taking the birth control pill to stop having lots more babies, not that she's ill.

Worried about Aids

I think my mum has Aids! I was in her room and found tablets in a sealed jar and a leaflet about Aids. I am so upset. Please help. Graham.

Answer

She could have that leaflet for all sorts of reasons – perhaps she wanted clear information for the day when you started asking questions about sex? Perhaps she went to the doctor for an ordinary check-up and picked up a leaflet in the surgery? Maybe she got it at the chemist's? Aids is a serious illness but quite hard to catch, thank God, and not many British women have fallen victim.

Grieving for lost brother

I'm a twelve-year-old girl who loves a seventeen-year-old boy. I have dreams about us both together. The problem is I'm not old enough to be his type of girlfriend. He was friendly with my brother aged sixteen who was killed last October. I don't think he remembers me. He reminds me of my brother. I don't know what to do. Harriet.

Answer

Nothing wrong in being friends, especially since you are linked by this tragedy. Perhaps it would be nice to talk about your brother with him from time to time – perhaps that's really why you like him?

Brothers and boyfriends

I'm going out with a boy a lot older than me. I'm twelve and he's nineteen. My parents don't know yet and I'm scared they will find out. I've got a love bite on my neck and my eighteen-year-old brother found out. He will only keep quiet if I dump this boy. Dawn.

Answer

Try to negotiate with your brother. Agree to stop snogging with this bloke but you have to be free to *talk* to your friends.

Boy wants more

There's a boy in my form at school who's always flirting with me. I didn't mind when it was fairly light-hearted – but it's getting heavier and more often. He's asked me out twice, but I refused as I've heard that relationships ruin friendships, and we are pretty good friends. However, he didn't stop even after I made it clear I wasn't interested that way, and it's very embarrassing. Some of my friends tease me about it – but I don't think it's funny. I don't have the nerve to tell him firmly to 'back off'. Any suggestions? Penny, thirteen, and upset.

Answer

Well, relationships may ruin friendships but some people would say relationships *include* friendships. However, it's your choice. If you really want him to stop pushing, you have to spell it out because the message did not get through before. Perhaps a note would be best – 'I like you as my friend and thanks for asking but I am *not* going out with you. See you tomorrow – XYZ'.

Too young to love?

I've got a big problem. I love girls but when I tell my mum and dad they make jokes about me and say not to get too serious (I'm ten). I am going out with a girl at the moment and I don't know when to kiss her. Nick.

Answer

Yes, I like girls too. I expect your dad feels the same way. If not, how did he ever meet your mum? Your parents are finding it hard to adjust to you growing up. I suggest you humour them. Let them pull your leg just a little. After all, you don't want to settle down too early. As for kissing, why not talk to your girlfriend? She's got a say in this too.

Sexy phone call

Please help, I'm dead worried. I rang one of those sexy stories for adults. I didn't think at the time, but the next day I saw this warning – 'These phone lines are of a sexually explicit nature – all calls at dialler's own risk'. Will the police get in contact with me? Help – Greg.

Answer

No, the police will not be involved unless your parents make a complaint. Even then, the phone service did issue a warning so I doubt whether any action would result. But remember – these calls are expensive so your mum and dad might start asking you awkward money questions.

How to tell parents 1

I have been going out with my boyfriend for seven weeks now but my parents don't know. I am fifteen and my boyfriend is twenty. I am afraid to tell my parents because I know that they won't approve because of the age gap. I am really fond of Pete, my boyfriend, and I'm not going to let my parents split us up. Seeing each other is a problem. Tuesdays and Thursdays he picks me up from school and we usually go back to his house until his mum and dad get in from work. We usually see each other once at the weekend. I tell my parents that I am going out with a girlfriend. I think my parents might be suspicious. Should I tell them about Pete or not? His parents don't know either. Miss 'X', West of England.

Answer

The age-gap is quite big now, which is why your parents may feel anxious, although it will seem less so in a couple of years' time. Living a set of lies is always difficult and when you get found out you appear to have been immature. If you're ready to prove that this relationship matters, then why not start by confiding in Pete's family? Tell them your worries and wishes. If they could approach your parents *with you*, there's a better chance that everyone will take you seriously and you'll get what you want.

How to tell parents 2

I fancy this girl who goes to a club that I go to. It was love at first sight for me. I didn't know how to tell her I loved her, so I started writing anonymous letters to her explaining the way I felt. She found out it was me somehow and told me she knew. I was very embarrassed. My problem is my parents. My dad especially. I could no way tell them I want to go out with a girl because I wouldn't have the guts and I know he won't approve. Don't get me wrong – he's a great person, but, well, you know. I expect you will tell me to sit them down and tell them straight, but I couldn't do it. Please tell me what to do. The girl and I are great friends and I buy her presents sometimes, but I just can't ask her out yet. I'm thirteen. David.

Answer

Maybe. But you *can* ask her round to do homework or lend you a book or play a computer game or help you dub a music tape. Anything to get your toe in the water. I don't think your dad will forbid you to have reasonable contact with another human being. And gradually he'll get used to the idea of you having *girl* friends. (You don't have to tell your parents that you're in love.)

Loves daddy

I know this sounds funny, but I have a hot spot for my dad and I am too shy to tell him. But I think he knows. It pleases him. Naomi, aged ten.

Answer

I'm sure your dad is aware that you admire him. That's great, and normal. You don't need to spell it out but if you want to say something, just tell him … he's great! (But you can't marry him – he's spoken for.)

Friend's boyfriend

I am thirteen and in love with my best friend's boyfriend. She has just had an argument with him and I am considering asking him out. Last week, he walked me and my friend home and then when we got to my house he kissed me. I want to know whether to ask him out or to leave it. Please help me. Anna – worried and in love.

Answer

If you ask him out without telling your best friend, she would probably never speak to you again. (Think of how you'd feel if the situations were reversed.) If you ask him out *after* telling your best friend she still may never speak to you again. You have to decide how important her friendship really is because there's certainly a chance that she might chuck you. So you decide if the risk is worth it. Find out how badly they are getting on, 'cos it's even possible she might be pleased to see the back of him.

Teased by sister

My sister's found out that I fancy this lad and she teases me. She keeps saying 'Make me a cup of tea or I'll tell everyone about the bloke you're mad on.' What should I do? Ignore my sister? Lose some fat and ask him out? Or forget about him? Lilly.

Answer

If you want to ask him out, do it. When your sister has a go, say 'Yes, I fancy him – so what? Don't you like boys?'

Blackmailed by sister

Recently my sister looked through my diary and found out who I fancy. She said that if I didn't give her a pound she would tell my mum and the boy I fancy, so I gave it to her. Now it has gone up to four pounds. What on earth can I do to stop it? Please help. Mandy.

Answer

Go and tell this boy that your sister is spreading silly rumours about you and him. This will also give you an opportunity to get better acquainted. Second, let your mum know you'd like to be friends with this boy because there's nothing wrong with it. Third, let your twister know you will tell both mum and dad what a scheming little blackmailer she is unless she gives back your five pounds at once.

Culture clash

I'm a young Asian girl. My parents are really strict. They never let me go out or do anything. Now my parents have arranged for me to get married to an Asian boy who lives in Pakistan. I don't want to marry him and I don't want to go to Pakistan. If I say no, they will kill me. I don't feel like staying at home any more but don't know where else to turn. Rani.

Answer

When you've been raised in Britain it's very hard to find your family still expects you to follow what may seem like 'foreign' rules. Don't despair – there's an Asian Family Counselling Service, on 081-997 5749, who can help.

Dead strange

We go to a boys' boarding school in south Oxfordshire and are fifteen. We share a study with another boy (whom we shall call Ollie) who's been acting quite strangely for the past two years. He claimed he could contact a dead relation by a seance and now we think he is in love with a lesbian teacher. We know this because he stares at her breasts and bottom and butters her up when he sees her. Should we do something about him? Anons.

Answer

Like what? Ollie may be a bit curious about the spirit world but seems to have a fairly normal interest in matters of the flesh. Women can, of course, look wonderful whatever their choice of partner.

Pesty boy

There's a boy at our school who's bothering us. He always seems to be talking about sex. Recently there have been rude notes put in our trays and they seem to come from him. He's ugly so we tell him to rack off but it makes him worse. What shall we do? Three Anons.

Answer

What you always do with the very young – don't expect too much grown-up behaviour. The human race has known about sex for thousands of years but he's only just discovered it. You don't need to say 'Rack off!' – just 'Dear, dear!'

Too old for sex?

Please can you help me? I'm a twelve-year-old girl. On Saturday morning I was downstairs watching TV, but I went upstairs again. My mum and dad were in their bed and when I walked in they threw themselves apart. I think they might have been having sex. I'm worried because both my parents are over forty. I'm too scared to ask Mum if they were having sex as I don't talk to her about things like that.

Answer

I sincerely hope your parents are as close and cuddly as you suspect. But even if they were being sexy, you didn't do any harm. They're old enough to cope and your embarrassment will soon pass. PS: there isn't an upper age-limit for sex.

Battle over boys

Recently I've started dating boys. At thirteen, I know I'm a little young but I'm very mature for my age. Last month, my mum found out and was furious to say the least. She read me the riot act and played the same old tune – 'school is more important at your age'. She's even banned me from seeing my boyfriend. I've tried to make her understand but she's too busy to listen since *her* boyfriend moved in with us. I feel confused and unwanted but I love her.

Answer

Then don't turn this into a battle. What's wrong with *combining* boys and homework? Keep getting good results and your mum can't moan. If the *real* problem is how you feel about *her* boyfriend, tell her you sometimes feel left out and insecure – can she help you with that?

Out of kilt

I'm a fifteen-year-old Scot and recently attended my sister's wedding. At the reception, the groom sneaked up behind me in the cloakroom and lifted up my kilt. I was really angry and embarrassed. He tried to make a joke out of it by saying he only wanted to see what I had on underneath. Some of his friends were there and they laughed as well. I never mentioned this to anyone at the time but do you think I should tell my sister? I never liked this man and if she knew what he did she'd feel differently about him too.

Answer

Getting humiliated by your brother-in-law at the reception was not the best of beginnings. He may be an oaf, he may have been drunk as a skunk but your sister won't leave him for playing a party prank. Telling her now can only make for bad blood between you. My advice is to be on hand if the marriage does go wrong but keep quiet in the meantime.

Lied to friend

I'm a twelve-year-old girl who's upset and confused and needs help. I lied to my best friend about something really awful and I don't know what to do about it. I told her that I've started my periods but I haven't. Do you think I should just be quiet and say nothing more about it until I do start, which I hope won't be long, or do you think I should tell her and apologize for lying to her? Please help. Victoria.

Answer

You could probably get away with lying but I have a hunch you'd feel dreadful about it. Telling your friend would not only be honest but could also improve your relationship. Funnily enough, she could really start to trust someone who could 'own up' to a mistake.

What a find!

Me and my friend found a condom in a boy's bag. Do not think we were being nosy but we were looking for a pen that he said we could borrow. What are we going to do? Laura.

Answer

Absolutely nothing. It isn't illegal to have one, it isn't your business and you don't want the school teasing him to death. I'm sure if the positions were reversed, you'd like *him* to keep quiet, wouldn't you?

Changing together

I'm eleven years old and I'd like to know if you think that it is wrong that the girls should change with the boys going to and coming back from PE? My class has to change together and all the girls hate it. It's not fair because some of us need to wear a bra. Please help. Chris.

Answer

I agree with you and think this is something you could discuss with mum and dad. See if they'd raise the subject with the head teacher at school. If enough parents object, I'm sure you could get the system changed.

Touchy teacher

I'm a thirteen-year-old girl and very mixed-up. The other day when I was in PE at school, my teacher kept on watching me. She kept me talking after gym so I was late for my shower. Everyone had finished by the time I got to the showers. My teacher said she'd give me a ride home afterwards. But when I had my shower, she helped to dry me off. My mum hasn't done this for some time now. What does this teacher want from me? Help. Tina.

Answer

Let's hope she was just being kind. But she clearly made you feel uncomfortable by touching your body even with a towel. I think it's very important you should feel free to say 'Thank you very much, I can dry myself.' Talk it over with mum.

Needs privacy

I have a really bad problem. It's my older brother. He keeps walking into my bedroom when I'm getting changed. I know it doesn't sound that bad but when your brother walks in on you and you are naked to the waist, it's very embarrassing. I'm really upset about it and I feel as if I'm going to die when I see him. Please help me with my problem. Helen.

Answer

Now you're becoming a woman you need more privacy. If big bruddy won't get the message, ask your parents for a small bolt for your door. This would stop unwanted intruders but could be broken if necessary in case of fire.

Loving father?

I'm a fifteen-year-old girl and my problem is my father. It's just that he always expects me to hold his hand, kiss him on the lips when I'm home from school, just basic things like that. He doesn't abuse me and has never advanced sexually, it's just that I feel this sort of action may lead him to get the wrong ideas. I'm too old for all this – what can I do to stop it? If I say anything, he ignores me or gets really mad and moody. Please help. Belinda.

Answer

There comes a time when it is no longer healthy to have such intimate contact with your father and he needs to respect your new womanhood. Give him your cheek to kiss instead. Put your affection into words – 'Hiya, Pop, have you had a good day?'

Kissing cousins

I'm a fourteen-year-old girl and very depressed. The other night I was at a party with all of my family there. Towards the end of the evening, I was talking to a boy who is my third cousin. Before he left, he kissed me. He'd had a few drinks. How will I find out if he really likes me or if he was drunk and can't remember?

Answer

Oh, I should think you'll have another opportunity to check this out. He's not going to Outer Mongolia. He probably won't kiss you the next time you meet, but if he *is* interested, there'll be furtive glances and the odd embarrassed smile and maybe a date. You've got to be *very* drunk to blank out totally.

Family love

Please help me. I am ten years old, the second of three girls. I really love my little sister but it's a family love. We play together. We do everything with each other. Sometimes I try to hug her and give her kisses but only as family. Because I do this, however, my older sister keeps on teasing me and saying I'm a lesbian. Am I? She goes on so much I'm almost beginning to think so. Triona.

Answer

Clear as day and bright as light I promise this doesn't make you a lesbian. If it did, then all the sisters in the world would be lesbians. Even if they fell out later on, most sisters in this country have shared the odd kiss especially when they were tots. I also think it's great that you like your younger sister so much because it's very easy to feel bothered by the arrival of your 'replacement' when the family is extended. Newborn babies need more care and attention than the older kids and the latter often show their jealousy and resentment by getting bitchy. I wonder if you know who I mean? I mention your older sister because you need to tackle her in two ways. First you have to understand why she might have mixed feelings about you because of your place in the family. Second, you need to learn how to survive her tedious teasing. Give Big Sis less incentive to feel left out. Try to spend a clear amount of time just with her and see if she'll come round. When you offer your goodnights to the family, don't exclude her – even if she's difficult for the time being. Try not to stir things up. Sometimes, we unconsciously 'enjoy' annoying and provoking people. If the three of you are out together don't pointedly favour Little Sis. When the dreaded L-word is trotted out, tell yourself 'I'm ready for that one' but don't reply. Smart comebacks like 'Takes one to know one!' only encourage the teaser to carry on. They know they've got you. It's better to change the subject, saying things like – 'What time's that programme on tonight that you want to see?' If you don't get provoked, the teasing won't work and she'll be forced to give up in the end.

Noisy parents

I'm a twelve-year-old girl and my room is beside my parents' bedroom. When my dad is off work, it is very easy to hear them making love. It doesn't seem to be much of a problem when you write it down but in fact I'm really getting upset. I want to approach them and tell them how I feel but I find it so difficult because they are my parents. What should I do? Cheryl.

Answer

First, full marks for asking the question. Your parents must have done a lot right to produce such a thoughtful daughter! Second, this is really about you growing up and becoming a young woman who is getting sexually conscious. Your parents have probably been making love in that room next to yours throughout the past twelve years but it's never bothered you before. What's new is how you think and feel about yourself. The changes in your own emotions are fascinating, but also mysterious, bewildering and worrying. When you think about your own body and how it works, the last image you want to pop into your mind is that of your mum and dad clasped in an embrace. Teenagers nearly always find it embarrassing to imagine their parents having sex, the people to whom they feel closest. But sex between your parents is right and proper, healthy and natural. You could thank your stars they betray a healthy lust for each other instead of moody indifference or the first stirrings of divorce. They have rights; you have rights. The question is how to reconcile them. Think hard whether it's possible to change bedrooms. If there's a spare room further away from your parents', ask if you could have it. You only need to say 'I'd like more peace and quiet.' Be reasonable – home's not a hotel. Don't fight unnecessary battles. If mum and dad predictably go to bed at five p.m. on a weekday, plan to be out of earshot in the kitchen or living room. If any major disturbance stops you getting to sleep, say after 9.30 at night, you're perfectly entitled to ask 'Please can you guys turn down the noise?' I know some kids who bang on the wall. Even if nothing changes, try to tune out. Sex is a very simple pleasure and (apart from celibates) everyone eventually does it.

Parents say no

I'm fifteen and a half and have been going steady with my boyfriend, Chris, for two years. He's a very grown-up seventeen. We've been on holiday together with both our families and have become an 'established' pair. The problem is that we want to sleep together and my parents are totally opposed to the idea. We feel ready (it's more by luck than anything else that I'm still technically a virgin). I've spent nights in his arms and know he's the right person for me. I want him to be the first one. But my parents insist it's wrong unless you're married. Bella.

Answer

They could also point out that until you're sixteen it's against the law. It might strengthen your case if you made it plain you will at least wait until after your next birthday. You describe your problem in an admirably mature way and that's how I'd encourage you to continue. In today's world, it's also refreshing to hear that you seek family approval. To get this, you need to convince your parents you are becoming old enough to make your own decisions. You also have to confront their deeply held moral beliefs. So begin by appreciating your parents' views as part of negotiating for what you want. The process of discussing these matters does alter people's attitudes and will assist your parents to think about you as more of a woman than a girl. Ask your parents to talk things over with Chris's parents. Perhaps all six of you could sit round the table? Have you any older brothers and sisters who could put in a good word as well? Or an aunt or uncle? Find out what your mum and dad worry about most – immorality, pregnancy or disease – and say you fully understand their anxieties. It's tough being a parent and it always was. Prepare answers that might reduce their worries. Contraception is easily arranged but you have to help organize it. On the moral issue, find out if you have common ground. For instance, could they *ever* bless your loss of virginity outside marriage, even at 28? Or 25? Or eighteen? Is the issue really sex before marriage, or 'thinking you're too young'? If there is absolutely no budge, point out that in two and a half years' time you can please yourself *and will*, but you'd prefer their support. How about it? Add that if they forbid you to express yourself sexually as a teenager, it is going to be a lot harder for you to make informed choices later on.

Embarrassing dad

When I am by myself or my friends come round, my dad always makes up jokes about sex and periods and he is really embarrassing. I try to ignore him and I usually go out of the room. Now I want to tell him how I feel but daren't for fear of hurting his feelings as he has always been a practical joker. Please tell me how I can let him know that I don't want him to make up any more jokes. Gabrielle.

Answer

Sometimes it's not just children who need to grow up. Parents can also find it difficult to realize more adult behaviour is required *from them*. Humour is a case in point. There are jokes and jokes and then there are practical jokes. Poking fun at every raw emotion is unkind. I think this is a way you can begin to approach your dad. You should show him that while it is acceptable to put a plastic spider in your cornflakes packet, it is not funny to make you feel dreadful about breasts and tampons. Because you are daunted by the changes of puberty, a word out of place here is actually *cruel*. What is damaged is your *image*. Explain that it's a bit like *you* laughing if *he* got made redundant. And he wouldn't like that! See your dad in a new light. Practical jokers are not all-powerful monsters but actually have trouble facing their own feelings. He also seems daunted by your sexual development. Tell him you like it when he makes fun *safely*. You don't want to swap him for a sobersides. Take him into your confidence. Can he *not* see that you are worried about your changing shape and appearance, not to mention your moods? Explain that your friends find him Over The Top. It won't hurt to serve up this home truth. Enlist your mum's help to reinforce your message. Be assertive when he's out of order – 'Dad, it's embarrassing, stop it!'

Black and white

I'm black and my boyfriend is white. We're both fifteen and live in south-east London. My family isn't racist but they would go mad if they found out about him. I can't tell my boyfriend that I'm not allowed out with white people because we love each other and I would be so upset if we broke up. Please can you help me and tell me what to do? I don't want to lose him, though. Delia.

Answer

Love means being able to tell him. Yes, people are prejudiced – most because they are white or pink; some because they are black. However, you can't solve this world problem by yourself. You can only be true to what you feel. If you don't say something to your boyfriend, how will you explain your absences? And if he can't support you through this difficult time, he's not going to be worth a lot. I know you are a bit torn but this is a time to start thinking and taking more decisions for yourself. Try to see this problem as something that might draw you together rather than pull you apart. So prepare the ground. Chat to your boyfriend about your family in general so he knows what you're up against. You need to have a discussion which won't be interrupted or end prematurely. Explain you're worried about losing *him*. Tell him straight out that your family is awkward. Can he understand you're going to have to keep him secret for a while? Allow him to feel rejected and even offended by this while stressing that you can understand these feelings. Repeat the most important thing – you *love* him. Then work out how and when to tell your family the truth. Maybe there's a more open-minded relative who could help you do this. If you're serious, the adults cannot stop you being in love.

Premenstrual mum

My mum gets suicidal once a month with dreadful PMS. She expects me to drop everything and do my rescue act, including most of the housework. I'm seventeen and I've got a right to my own life. How can I get her off my back? All the doctor tells her is to take vitamins. Michelle.

Answer

Obviously you'd like your mother to enjoy better health. And you wouldn't have a problem if she didn't suffer from PMS (pre-menstrual syndrome), so it's in your very best interest to help her get well. Facts: as many as 40 per cent of women aged between fifteen and fifty experience PMS. Six of the most common symptoms are irritability, depression, breast pain, bloating, headaches and clumsiness. A sufferer can feel fat and ugly, have an evil temper and a sense that life is not worth living. The condition is not a joke and if men had to put up with half of these problems they'd have found a cure in 1066 BC. I hope you have misrepresented the approach of your mum's GP. In addition to taking vitamin B6 (Pyridoxine), she perhaps needs specialist help. This may involve drawing up a 'hormone profile' as well as possible drug treatment. Give your mum the good news that doctors can do more than offer vitamins. Encourage your mum to keep a 'Menstrual Diary' so that when she sees a consultant, she has a useful record of each symptom and its intensity. Tell her that Efamol (evening primrose oil) has been medically proved to help in over 60 per cent of cases of PMS, with symptoms reduced by up to 95 per cent. (Full information in Judy Graham's book *Evening Primrose Oil*, published by Thorsons, which you could give her as a present.) Find out if other worries tend to tip your mum 'over the edge' each month. Perhaps these could be tackled in advance on her good days? Say that you're willing to do your fair share of chores at home and even more when she's ill. But not if she refuses to seek help for her condition. That's what's unfair.

Culture clash

I am sick of being treated like a baby. I'm sixteen, nearly seventeen, but my parents won't let me go out with a boy in my class I'm really fond of. He is a different religion from us (we're Jewish, but don't practise). They allowed me out with him for one night when I threatened to leave home, but they say that's the limit. Now they threaten to stop me going to college if I don't comply with their wishes. I love them but what can I do? Miriam.

Answer

Recognize how difficult this problem is. You are not only coping with adolescence, like your schoolfriends, but facing a battle of cultures. Your family's religion is struggling with modern ways of courting. You also need to see how very much you are piggy in the middle. Even though your parents don't go to a synagogue, they have given you the message that sexual mixing is wrong. At school, you've probably been given the opposite view. This contradiction is hardly your fault. But rather than hope to satisfy everyone, brace yourself to choose the way that feels right for you. You may have to opt for 'the lesser of two evils'. Family *beliefs* cannot be argued away so don't try. You're on better ground if you attempt to allay your parents' *anxieties* about losing you. Get them to put their darkest fears into words while you show you really understand what they are saying. Don't retaliate – let them sound off. They won't be able to negotiate until they have calmed down. The more you sound mature, the harder they will find it to treat you like a child. Then make your points. Say you understand their feelings. Can they understand yours? Remind them that you did go out with this boy for a whole evening without a disaster. Point out that pressure tactics will destroy your relationship with them. Is this what they want? Say they *could* be right about this boy but you need to find out for yourself. They are actually forcing you to want him more, not less. If they care for your protection, tell them you must learn to make your own decisions now. Otherwise you will be vulnerable to any old cheat and liar when they are no longer around to advise. Going to college usually means leaving home. Remind them they must soon stop running your social life anyway. If they are still resistant, decide whether to bite the bullet. You *know* it works when you talk about moving out. Tell them quietly they are driving you to plan for independence sooner than you expected. Can they shift on this issue, or are they asking you to find a flat instead of a place at college?

Mum's abortion

My mum is having an abortion and she won't tell my dad. I'm really upset about this and don't know what to do. Help. Andrew, thirteen.

Answer

It's unfair that you have been told this, especially when your dad hasn't. It's not a son's job to cope with his parents' emotions – they should be coping with yours. Obviously your mum is short of adult friends with whom to share her worries. She is someone who can be tempted into using her children for this purpose, but you need to resist. This is serious. Unless you can get the message across that the grown-ups should literally mind their own business, you're likely to be faced with more of the same in the future. The danger here is that you will interrupt your own growing-up process in order to parent her. Even in terms of solving mum's problem, it's bad news. If she has major disagreements with your father, they won't be settled by constructing a web of domestic secrecy. In addition, it may be irrational, but I am sure you are beginning to wonder whether she wanted to have *any* children, including you. Tell your mum you realize she is anxious but she must understand so are you. It scares you to be told things for which you can't take responsibility. It fills you with a kind of helpless guilt. Explain how you need to stay friends with both your parents whatever she may be going through. In future, could she promise not to ask you to keep bad secrets which force you to take sides? If it helps, point out that life-and-death secrets shouldn't be shared anyway. To keep something completely secret, silence is paramount. You can't be expected never to blurt out something by accident. You might also remind her you haven't grown up yet, let alone become a birth counsellor. Who else could she talk to about all this? Could you finally have some reassurance about your own future?

Worried about sister's reputation

My youngest sister (sixteen) is getting keen on a boy whom I know to be really awful – you know, the sort who boasts about his sexual conquests. What can I do? Maggie.

Answer

You have a choice. If you warn your sister off, she will

probably resent you for months as well as flinging herself into the arms of an unworthy lover. If you bite your tongue, she may still make a painful mistake but it will be entirely hers and one from which she can learn. Whatever the outcome, the helpful course is for you to be supportive. If she does have a hard time, you can do your best to introduce her to other young men who are not compiling their erotic memoirs.

Promiscuous mother

My parents divorced five years ago when I was fourteen and since that time my mother must have had twenty lovers. I'm always finding her in bed with someone or other and our house resembles a bus station. I am worried it will make me promiscuous too. Stephanie.

Answer

You may simply feel worried full stop. The uncertainty created by this situation must be confusing for you. But one of the sad facts of divorce is that the family can never be the same afterwards and your mother's behaviour seems to have settled into a pattern. What you really need is an area of peace, stability and privacy. Put a lock on the door of your room so you feel secure in there. Work out a sensible routine for the time you spend in the house so you can make life more predictable. Tell your mother about your distress so that even if she carries on as before, she might consider not disturbing you so much, or making you meet all her friends. Other options would include going to live with your father if he can have you. As for your potential promiscuity, this experience is as likely to make you monogamous as polygamous. In other words, the whole situation is making you anxious but you remain in charge of your future love-life. That hasn't changed.

Competitive mum

I have been brought up in a one-parent family by my mother who is still quite young and we often do things together. Now a new manfriend seems to be preferring me to her and I can see she is eaten up with bad feeling. I can't handle this. Trish.

Answer

When all is said and done she is your mother, not your sister. It sounds as if she has the roles confused and maybe you do too. If the man is her friend, in her age group, I suggest you bow out. If, on the other hand, he is of your generation, and you say he prefers you, why should you give him up? Your mother seems to feel competitive with you and however super a person she is, needs to get on with her own life and allow you to fashion yours. Try putting more distance into the relationship for both your sakes.

Liberal parents

My parents are too bloody liberal. They told my girlfriend last night that she was welcome to be 'private' with me in their house any time. The implication was definitely to do what they call 'bonking'. They make me sick. My girlfriend was extremely embarrassed since we haven't got anywhere near that stage yet. How can I control them? Richard.

Answer

Perhaps by explaining to them, as you have to me, that their 'over-the-top', slightly 60s approach, has impeded your love-life rather than enhanced it.

Smartie dog

I have a dog called Smartie and he normally sleeps on my bed. One morning I woke up and Smartie was on top of me. I usually sleep without clothes on because it's hot in our house. Is it possible that I'm pregnant from my dog? Please give me some advice. Sincerely, a very worried eleven-year-old Gwynneth.

Answer

No. It's biologically impossible.

One-man rule

I'm a fourteen-year-old girl and I'm just so depressed. I have a boyfriend who lives 200 miles away. I lost my virginity to him and I really regret it. My mum read my diary and found out. She went mad and made me feel really guilty. I couldn't believe she'd read my diary. I went off my boyfriend and dumped him, but my mum kind of forced me to go back out with him again. She really likes him and she thinks you should only sleep with one man. I'm sure she wants me to marry him. She makes me feel like a slag and I'm not. I really don't want to see him again because I know he'll want to have sex. From Sarah.

Answer

If it was a mistake, put it behind you and don't let anyone decide who you will or won't love and marry. That's *your* decision.

Boyfriend spreading rumours

I'm a thirteen-year-old and have been going out with a twelve-year-old boy for two months now. Recently we've been talking about having sex. We decided not to as I didn't want to lose my virginity at such a young age. I thought this would be OK and we could keep going the way we were. I was wrong! The next day at school I found out that he had told nearly everybody in the school that we had actually had sex! I'm really pissed off and I'm the laughing stock of the school. Please help! I need it! Gail.

Answer

Have a quiet chat with this lad and tell him if he doesn't stop spreading these lies you will start a few rumours about him. He'll know the sort I mean.

Blackmailing sister

I have a boyfriend who I really love. Our relationship is solid, and although I'm under the age of consent (I'm fifteen) I have slept with him several times. The problem is my sister has found out and is blackmailing me. She's said she'll tell my parents unless I pay her £20 a week. My parents are really old-fashioned about the law and would stop me from seeing him if they knew. Amelia.

Answer

Tell her you'll cut her out of your life if she behaves like such a scumbag.

Brother's problem

My brother got a girl pregnant and my mum and dad are taking it out on me. They keep saying I'm a failure and I'm no good at anything. They never help me with my school work. I'm thirteen now and it's an important time in my life to see if I get to a clever school or not. I don't think so as this is affecting my school work. I'm not allowed out anywhere unless I'm with my mum. Mum keeps reading my diary to see what I'm up to. It's been going on for three weeks now. I can't stick it any longer. It's getting to me. I wish I was dead. I need help. Joan.

Answer

Tell them what you've told me – you are *not* your brother. Don't leave your diary around for your mum to read – that's outrageous anyway. If she insists, then stop writing it. Your parents are overreacting because of your brother, but it won't last for ever. If they say you're a failure, reply 'Could you try encouraging me, then?'

Friend with BO

We have a problem with one of our friends. She is indescribably unclean. She smells like she has never washed. We don't want to tell her this because she will get upset and won't like us any more. This is no joke. We really need some advice. What should we do? From two friends.

Answer

If you say it sensitively, you can tell anyone anything. Just explain that there is a problem and people are commenting so perhaps she could get a stronger deodorant? We *all* smell, after all.

Barry the chimp

We're very concerned about our two best friends. They have an imaginary friend called Barry. He is a chimp and has a dirty mind. In our lessons Barry is up our skirts and down our shirts. Last week we had a young, good-looking teacher for games because our usual teacher was away. During the lesson Barry had been down her shirt and done sexual things. We are concerned. From two friends.

Answer

Imaginary friends are useful when you feel shy or embarrassed – they can do things you daren't. But Barry will soon be forgotten when your friends start dating boys for themselves. Try not to worry.

Licking condoms?

The other night I went to a pub bonfire and in the toilets there was a condom machine. My friends and I could not help getting some. We licked them and they tasted disgusting. We didn't know what to do with them so we flushed them down the loo. We are only ten years old. Will we be all right? From four very worried girls.

Answer

Condoms are *not* poisonous and you will come to no harm.

Brotherly love

I am very worried. One day my brother and I got on his bed and started kissing. Another day we were playing and I pulled my gown off and we kissed. I now realize this is silly and feel very guilty. I'm scared. He keeps wanting to do it again. My brother is seven. Help! Agnes.

Answer

Just tell him no – the game is over.

Brother taking advantage

I went out with my mum and dad to take my dog for a walk. My friend came and knocked for me. My brother opened the door and said I'd gone out but would be back soon, but he knew I wouldn't be back for ages. My friend went in and waited. My brother asked her if she wanted to come up and play on his computer, which she did. While she was playing he went in the bathroom and came back naked. Then he started to undress her. When I came home I went upstairs and I heard a noise coming from my brother's room. I peeped through the keyhole and there was my brother on top of my friend. He was holding her down and kissing her and making love to her. Now my friend is pregnant. She's fourteen. Anon.

Answer

Then you need to be a good friend to her. She'll need to talk to the grown-ups, including the doctor, and you also need to find out whether your brother forced his attentions on her. If so, he's in a lot of trouble. Go with her to the local Brook Advisory Service so she can get pregnancy counselling. The national phone number is 071-708 1234.

Planning ahead

We are going on a school journey soon and some boys want to share a room with us. When we asked why, they said they wanted to get off with us. We've all started our periods and are worried something might happen. What should we do? We don't want to end up pregnant. From four very worried girls.

Answer

Then have a word with the teacher about the sleeping arrangements. I'm sure there'll be some supervision and you could call out if there were a problem.

Needs to talk

My problem is not what's happening now, but what's happened throughout my childhood. I have a mentally handicapped brother who's two years younger than myself, so as a child I was pushed from pillar to post as he was often having stays in hospital, and everything we did depended on him. This didn't bother me – I just matured quickly and got on with things. My dad is an alcoholic and I give up a lot of my time to help my mum with my brother as my dad's never around, and when he is he's always drunk. Between the ages of eleven and sixteen I was also sexually abused by a member of my family but I've always just shut this out and got on with life. Now I'm almost eighteen and will be going to university soon, but all the feelings I've shut out keep coming back and I feel like an insecure five-year-old.

I've never really been close to my family so I can't talk it over with them. I'm just so confused. Anon.

Answer

These dark feelings need to come out. Why not contact a group called Family Matters, who counsel the survivors of sexual abuse, on 0474 537392?

Lovebites and dad

My boyfriend and I get carried away and covered in lovebites. My dad says I'm a whore but I've never had intercourse.

Answer

Your father sounds jealous as well as obnoxious but if keeping the peace at home is important for a few more years ask your boyfriend to confine his lovebites to your less public regions.

Sex talk

My ten-year-old brother is just learning about sex in school. The thing is that he always seems to bring the subject up when I'm around, especially when we are all having our tea and I can't get away from it. It's not that I'm embarrassed about it – or maybe I am? – but I just *hate* discussing it. Then my mum will say something like 'I think she's embarrassed' and makes fun of me. I pretend not to be listening but then my dad will say, 'I bet she's taking it all in though.' This really hurts me and when I think of all my personal problems that I've discussed with my mum it hurts even more when she makes fun of me. Lately I've been shutting myself away in my room so as to avoid the situation but I can't do that for ever. I really can't talk to my parents about it but I don't know what to do. Please help. Anon, aged fourteen.

Answer

These family teatimes are making you very self-conscious. I think it's worth having one more stab at telling mum you feel really knotted with embarrassment by them and betrayed when she joins in. Please could she be a little more sensitive to your feelings?

Crush on P H

We're worried about our friend. She has a crush on you. Every picture she can find of you goes on her wall. Just lately she has only been thinking of you. She got told off by our teacher for daydreaming. She always talks in her sleep about you. She plays silly games where she ends up marrying you. We've written seven times before. Please answer as it has got worse. From Two Sisters.

Answer

Well, I didn't get the other six letters so lord knows where you've sent them. I'm glad to be of use to your friend. We all need crushes to practise our feelings on and I don't think she'll come to any harm. The whole point of a crush is that it's safe – you don't have to meet the other person or put up with their grotty side since you are *imagining* what they are like and how they'll be.

9

What Parents Need to Ask

Finally, a few words of helpful encouragement for your parents. If mum or dad sometimes doesn't know how to cope with you, perhaps they'll find some answers in this chapter? The main problem for both sides is to respect the other's needs and feelings. A wise man once said that being a parent is the world's most difficult job and you always end up making mistakes. My kids have been very forgiving and I'm glad we stay good friends. I hope you can do as much for your oldies.

When to tell

When should my daughter know the facts of life? I am worried that talking about sex will encourage experiments with sex. Grace.

Answer

When do you tell the facts of life? As soon as your child

is old enough to understand them. Really the question should be turned round – 'Are there any good reasons for depriving my daughter of this important information?' However, you must always proceed at the child's own pace, in the child's own language. So when your three-year-old asks where babies come from, do not deliver a lecture on the more advanced chapters of the *Kama Sutra*. It makes most sense to discuss the facts of life when the child is about two or two and a half in response to a question or as part of bedtime reading. Provided you are a reasonably approachable parent, your child *will* ask you questions about sex at some time when aged between two and four. Teaching a child specifically about how the genitals work, again following some question or other, is more appropriate at the age of six or seven. Girls in particular need this type of education. Bathtime offers a good opportunity for Mum to lend a mirror and explain the function of the different parts. Again there are lots of books that can fill any gaps in your own knowledge. My worry is that you may have left things till your daughter has reached puberty. Perhaps your own family was silent on this subject so you have been the same? If this is true, she now needs help to catch up. Be assured that information isn't 'encouragement'. Describe the practicalities of love, sexual safety and contraception while making your own moral views clear. Marshal your arguments. You can say something like 'The Pill is thought to be the best contraceptive but I believe schoolchildren are not ready for a sexual relationship.' Send a stamped s.a.e. to the FPA, 27-35 Mortimer Street, London W1N 7RJ for a copy of *Healthwise*, their mail-order books catalogue listing all the educational texts which will simplify your task.

Prudish son

My fourteen year-old son is incredibly prudish. He's shocked by topless pin-ups, bad language and tells us off if we crack a saucy joke or laugh suggestively. What's happened? Gail.

Answer

You almost said 'Where have we gone wrong?' and the answer is that children get influenced by many people besides their parents. Think about it. Are their grandparents holding these opinions? Or teachers? Or preachers? Or TV evangelists? Or other mentors or friends? Or books of doctrine? You must also think about your own beliefs. Have you tried to ram 'permissiveness' down your child's throat with the predictable response that he is 'rebelling' against your values?

Is he too young?

My fourteen-year-old son seems extraordinarily inter-ested in girls. Surely he's too young? Agnes.

Answer

You may not have noticed, but children grow up earlier than they did even ten years ago. Some girls are starting their periods at nine or ten (each decade the average age of onset falls by one month) and both sexes are fashion-conscious by this stage. Then again, the age of consent for sex and marriage in English-speaking countries was as low as twelve in the last century. So do you really think your son's behaviour all that strange? Get to know him better.

Too old for cuddles

My thirteen-year-old daughter still comes to bed with us for a cuddle in the morning. I think she is too old for this now but my husband disagrees. Am I wrong? Rita.

Answer

You are right. Girls generally reach sexual maturity two years earlier than boys and twelve/thirteen is the average age for the commencement of menstruation. At this point, your daughter is rapidly becoming a sexual adult and it is no longer appropriate for her to have such confusing bodily contact with her father in the marital bed. I don't mean you should start a touching taboo – just keep it out of suggestive locations in nightclothes.

What's wrong with him?

My sixteen-year-old son continues to show absolutely no interest in the opposite sex at all. Should I be worried? Dee.

Answer

I take it you mean he shows no 'interest' in the same sex either, and that you are specifically concerned about his unenthusiasm for heterosexual romance? I suggest you are still jumping the gun. Your concern might be justified in three or four years' time but it will always be his battle, not yours, since you cannot arrange for him to have your feelings. (Even if his inclinations are gay, these may not be established for many months ahead).

What to do

I found a condom in my fourteen-year-old daughter's pocket. What should I do? Beryl.

Answer

Perhaps first of all breathe a sigh of relief that if she is precocious enough to be sexually active, she is also precocious enough to protect herself from pregnancy – you hope. But of course it is never safe to make assumptions. As her legal guardian, as well as her friend, you need to know what, if anything, is going on. Choose a good time to talk calmly, then tell her what you've found. Even if she says she was given it in the school playground, use the opportunity to discuss what condoms are for and why they are thought to be a good idea. This might let you hear what she thinks about the subject of sleeping with boyfriends. If she turns out to be sleeping with hers, you need to know more before taking decisions. What sort of guy is he? Is this a steady relationship (even at fourteen), or a passing fancy? Can she deal with it, or is she under heavy pressure? Is she defiant and blasé, or do you see her, possibly for the first time, as more grown-up? Does she seem to be using her relationship as compensation in some way, or is it sweetly loving? In effect, is she crying out for help or just getting on with life? When you've got these answers you'll know what you need to do. Please remember that some teenagers are mature beyond their years. Think about the consequences of any laws you may lay down. A negotiated compromise to which all parties agree might be your best outcome.

I think he's gay

I think my seventeen-year-old son may be homosexual. Should I tell him I suspect? Adam.

Answer

Unless you've got a special reason leading you to suppose your son may come to harm it would be better to leave any revelations up to him. First, he may not feel ready to talk about it yet. Second, there is presumably a chance that you've got it wrong on what could be a very sensitive subject for him. What you could do constructively is show by the way you talk about homosexuals and sexual identity that you are not a rejecting person while also confirming from time to time how much you love him.

Is my daughter gay?

My seventeen-year-old daughter always seems to be hugging her schoolfriend. Does this mean she's a lesbian? Hilda.

Answer

Probably not, since women have always been permitted to behave more demonstrably together than (Anglo-Saxon) men. There are phases in adolescence when girls become so involved with their friends that they quite literally can't leave them alone. A minority of girls may turn this into something erotic, or para-sexual. Yet it may still be mainly a friendship 'frenzy'. Although some lesbian women are aware of their sexual identity early in life, others don't find it out until their twenties and thirties. If you think the kids are going too far, you might say 'I understand it, but others may not', though I still get the feeling that the discomfort is primarily yours.

Homosexuality – a 'cure'?

Can you cure a child of homosexuality? Peter.

Answer

No, because it is not a disease and for more than a decade now the governing body of US psychiatry has concluded for its members that homosexuality is indicative of no type of 'pathology'. In the fifties and sixties, however, the story was different, and punitive psychologists were prepared to offer 'aversion therapy' as a serious cure. However, this treatment made homosexual arousal painful rather than converting gays into straights. One homosexual whom doctors attempted to convert was made to drink salt water every time he had a gay fantasy. The only result was that he felt seasick.

Caught in the act

I found my eighteen-year-old on the sofa having sex with his girlfriend. Was I right to be angry? Ian.

Answer

That depends on your background and morality. If you have been conditioned to think this sort of behaviour sinful, unethical or bad-mannered, it's no surprise that you lost your cool. If the vision raised uncomfortable sexual feelings too – perhaps of jealousy or envy, even lust – then you might well experience rage to cope with them. Possibly you felt territorial? 'How dare they invade my relaxation space with their condoms and love stains?' I can appreciate how you might react. But the important question is what you are going to do next, because whatever has happened to you, there are two young people who are now feeling rather embarrassed and distressed? Could you let them realize what a shock you got and gently suggest that you do understand their need to love, even though family living rooms make inadequate boudoirs?

Daughter's abortion

My teenage daughter is depressed after an abortion. What can she do? Audrey.

Answer

Nothing in a hurry. She has got to sail through an ocean of sad feelings. You can help by talking about a life that might have been and a future she couldn't make happen. She may also have difficult thoughts about the man who made her pregnant, about her inability to avoid tough choices, together with thoughts about any other major past losses which this event will almost inevitably recall. It may also be a good move to suggest she talks things over with a professional counsellor, many of whom now offer a special service in relation to abortion.

Health risks

Apart from Aids, is it true there are special health risks for a teenager who is sexually active? Mandy.

Answer

There appears to be a greater chance of teenagers

acquiring herpes or genital warts and the youthful cervix is apparently more vulnerable to viral attack than that of the fully mature female. Both herpes and warts, therefore, involve an increased long-term risk of uterine cancer. If either is contracted, six-monthly cervical smears should be taken.

Disapproves of daughter's dress sense

My sixteen-year-old daughter dresses like a tart. She knows this upsets me but refuses to change. Louise.

Answer

Your daughter, like any other adolescent, is trying to find her own personal style, sexual and otherwise. She may be getting this a little wrong, perhaps over-the-top, but sometimes we feel we can only learn by taking things to extremes. At least, she can feel comfortably sure she's found a fashion identity that you'd never be seen dead in, so in her terms, she's successfully 'created a new person separate from Mum'. But further, she seems to be on the one hand attractive, and on the other dramatic. This probably means there is a part of her which feels the opposite – less attractive and not very significant. Confidence is a fragile plant at the best of times and thoughtless parents can easily destroy it. If you could congratulate her when she pleases you but remain mute when you think she's got it wrong, you will do more to help her form sensible judgements than if you constantly nag. A girl's revealing her panties like a tart may be a misguided method of proving herself sexually attractive, and therefore lovable, but she has to discover for herself that lovability does not come from sexual availability. Your tragedy is that if you tell her how to live you may destroy her capacity to do so.

Maturing son

My son has taken to spending hours in the bathroom. I suspect from the evidence he is masturbating. Should I say anything? Davina.

Answer

No, that would be rude, unless you or the family need to use the room and can't because the door is always locked. If this is your only bathroom, I suggest you ask him not to occupy it during rush hour(s).

More cuddles

My sixteen-year-old's idea of a cuddle is to press his whole body against me. I want to hug him back but will he get the wrong idea? Tessa.

Answer

Sons need cuddles from their mums at most ages although some respond more demonstratively than others. However, when they start seeing women as sex objects, in early teenage, you should begin to alter the way in which cuddles are received. If he presses his whole body against yours, move slightly sideways to avoid his full frontal. Begin the habit of putting an arm round his shoulder and hugging him from the side. A goodbye hug and kiss can still be managed with heads and shoulders pressed close but other regions held apart. He'll pick up the message which is quite a good one to hear – that you now acknowledge his sexual status while continuing to offer him your complete affection.

Promiscuous daughter?

My daughter has a new boyfriend every month and this worries me. Will she ever settle down? Paul.

Answer

You can console yourself with the thought that practically everyone who can be married does get married. They may not stay with the same person for life, and they may not be married when you want them to be, but the human race still strives after this estate. Perhaps your daughter is checking out all the possibilities because she knows how important it is to pick a winner? Or more subtly, perhaps she realizes she must work through a lot of personal experience before being able to offer a man a mature partnership? If she shows genuine signs of depression or self-dislike, the problem is different and you could try to probe the wound – otherwise surgery is not called for. Would you worry so much if she were a son?

Love and sex

I'd like my kids to think that the best sexual relationships are built on love. Am I hideously old-fashioned? Glenda.

Answer

You are romantically acknowledging the special quality possessed by loving relationships which become sexual. But there are fine unions based on different assumptions: the relationship that is poignant when 'ships pass in the night', perhaps in wartime; the relationship which is pure comedy; one based on friendship where flirtation flares into passion. Another when colleagues at work fall into each other's arms after a campaign triumph. One based on curiosity, when a teenager needs to know 'what it will be like', and many more – all these can be excellent sexual experiences in their own right.

Married lover

I have read my daughter's diary and she is having an affair with a married man. She is not yet eighteen. Should I intervene? Paula.

Answer

If your daughter wanted you to know about the affair she would have confided in you. If she is otherwise behaving normally, I would think it important to respect her privacy, independence and even her 'right to make possible mistakes'. A seventeen-year-old is a virtual adult and needs to be recognized as such. The fact that you are reading her diary shows you have not so far done this. The only time to interfere would be if she were obviously distressed and needing help.

In love with teacher

My fourteen-year-old daughter has fallen in love with her school chemistry teacher. I found this out by glancing at her diary. She describes lying in wait in the school corridor just to catch a glimpse of him. I am very worried in case this matter gets out of hand. What would you advise me to do? Naomi.

Answer

I'd suggest you ask yourself what you can do? First, it

will be difficult to reveal your source of knowledge without appearing in a poor, rather snooping light. I don't suppose you want to teach your child that spying is moral or that confidences should be betrayed. Second, you don't know whether what you read was fact, fiction or a healthy wish-mixture of the two. I know from the letters sent to me by teenagers that they can't all have talked to Michael Jackson or Kylie Minogue in the street as they claim. (Especially in Southampton, Bolton and Wrexham on the same Friday.) Third, it's utterly normal to form what we call in the trade 'transitional crushes' – falling for unattainable adults in safety before we're ready to expose ourselves to reality. Part of growing up is choosing role models outside the family to test our feelings on. Ditto for values (she needs to compare your beliefs with those of other admired grown-ups). Fourth, chemistry teachers are experts on … chemistry. He'll have dealt with this before. (He's probably the most handsome of the men teachers at school, or gives off an aura of strength or vulnerability and correspondingly is attractive.) Last, so long as you remain a good, supportive, listening mum (who doesn't impersonate a police officer) you will know whether your daughter's ever in moral danger or not. So make sure the lines of communication remain open – even if it means you have to sit together through a few episodes of her favourite soap opera to stay in touch.

What do I tell him?

My fourteen-year-old son Mark is working hard at school and as far as I know hasn't any sexual experience but what should I tell him about early and pre-marital sex? I'm not a prude but I don't want to encourage experiments by saying the wrong thing. I still wish young people could wait till they were married. Linda.

Answer

I'm sure you are no prude and could hold an adult conversation with anyone about the facts of life. I bet you've been known to smile at the odd risqué joke too, because we all do that sometimes, don't we? All the same, you are clearly not very comfortable with the brave new world of active teenage sexuality. Partly, this will be a direct result of 'things your mother taught you', especially those things that your mother told you personally *not* to do. It is very difficult to challenge the 'voices of our education' especially on a subject regarded with such importance by so many for so long. However, when your mother was growing up (practising what *she* was taught in the 1930s!) there was no contraceptive pill, no legal abortion, no sex education and no soap opera on TV. It may not be a better world today, but it is a very different one in which many teenagers know as much about sex as we do. My postbag from children's television, for instance, is choc-a-bloc with letters from girls of ten who want to know how to get a steady boyfriend, how to kiss and when their periods will start. By the age of eleven, the boys are asking for similar information. Even ten years ago, things were different (my older sons, for example, were not interested in girls, or personal hygiene, till they were in their mid-teens). So the question has to be put – can we apply your mother's rules to today's teenagers? I think the answer is something like – well, you can try, but expect to compromise because your son has to live in a world where his friends and peers are very sexually knowing and he has to get along with them, rather than with the people who educated your

mum who are long since dead. In any case, the age of
consent to sex and marriage varies throughout Europe
so we have to accept there's a flexibility about when
adulthood begins.

Your other concern is with Mark's schoolwork. Will
girls get in the way of study and exams, you seem to
say? The answer here is 'to some extent', whatever you
tell him about sex (though research into co-education
suggests that boys are far less distracted by the
presence of the opposite sex than girls). The facts of
biology are going to make him pass some time
'erotically', whether alone mooning about Madonna or
in the real-life company of a junior passion.

Parents can't win – your best bet is to wait and see
how he would like to live his personal life rather than
tell him what to do in advance. As to what you say, I
think it's a parental obligation to offer accurate
information about feelings, sexual facts, contraception
and the risks from modern viruses. (If you want written
help, the Brook Advisory guide *Say Yes, Say No, Say
Maybe*, is available from the Brook Education Centre, 24
Albert Street, Birmingham B4 7UD). Above all, I think
you should make it absolutely clear that you have
strong personal opinions. You could start, 'I think sex is
beautiful but you may get very hurt and confused by it
if you try to sleep with someone before you can cope
with the possible emotional side-effects – jealousy,
possessiveness, despair and a broken heart ... not to
mention an unplanned pregnancy.' You can make this
speech while at the same time talking freely about what
others do, and without introducing prohibitions. The
best teaching is by example and I'm sure Mark will
respect you most if you display a calm quiet confidence
in your own point of view.

He's growing up

My thirteen-year-old son, Peter, has had a girlfriend for three weeks. I find myself completely unable to come to terms with this. When I was a teenager, this didn't happen until lads were at least sixteen. If he were older, I could discuss what this means – things like contraception, safe sex, responsibility etc. But how do I talk to a child about running a love life? Kate.

Answer

It seems like yesterday that your son was learning to walk. As children grow up, parents naturally find it harder to keep pace. From schooldays onward, we are less involved in their waking lives. We have to ask them what's happening when we're not around. When you take into account the fact that society is also changing all the time, it's no wonder we get caught out. I think most parents feel a sense of shock and surprise when their children enter puberty. And most mums have trouble seeing their young sons on the arms of girls. So your reaction is not bizarre. One mum I know shed a tear the other day when her twelve-year-old said, 'Can we put the cuddly toys away in the cupboard because they clutter up my bed?' Parents lose as well as gain from the changes in children's lives. Your first response is heartfelt – an overwhelming sense of wanting to shout No. Don't worry. That's what we usually say before tackling an inevitably difficult task. In fact, physical puberty in boys has always started at about the age of eleven or twelve. The male sex hormone testosterone gets to work, growth speeds up, the shoulders and chest get broader, the penis becomes thicker and longer, the voice breaks, erections occur at inconvenient moments, pubic hairs grow, wet dreams happen, masturbation starts and the whole process may be crowned with pimples.

In the last century, people could actually marry at the age of twelve, so teenage was less of a problem. I think things were harder when you and I were young because we generally expected to wait until we were sixteen to twenty before dating and mating. If you think back, you might recall this as a time of strain. I do. The impact of sex hormones is immensely powerful. And so we really had to wrestle with our dreams and longings to control our desires. Today, under the impact of television programmes like *Neighbours, Home and Away, Byker Grove* and *Grange Hill*, I suspect young people are really catching up with themselves again. Their desire to go on a first date is better synchronized with their physical development. As you are quick to realize, whatever problems this solves, it also creates new emotional dilemmas for parents as well as their children. Obviously, as a society, we don't approve of sex at thirteen. It remains illegal. The role for parents is to establish that while kissing and cuddling feel great at any age, going all the way is 'wrong' when you are too young to handle pregnancy, paternity or rejection by a sex partner. The best way to get the message across at home is not to ban Peter from seeing his girlfriend. Instead, why not sit down with him while he watches these TV programmes about young love and discuss the plots? I think it would be much easier for you to ask him, 'What would you do if … a friend of yours got pregnant?' in front of *Neighbours* on the box than deliver any lecture in cold blood. You could then go on to negotiate some family rules about staying out late, doing homework, kissing in front of granny and so on. And in case it feels quite overwhelming, let me add that teenage does pass. In five years' time Peter will be old enough to vote.

Ex-boyfriend problems

My eighteen-year-old daughter Claire is plagued by an ex-boyfriend who keeps ringing her day and night, although she has finished with him. She wants me to keep intercepting the calls and say she isn't in. I'm as anxious as she is for these calls to stop – but I don't feel this is the way. Any suggestions? Doris.

Answer

Possibly Claire wants to avoid a confrontation by getting you to do her 'dirty work' for her. Quite rightly, you would say this isn't your job. If she has not said goodbye to her boyfriend in words of one syllable, she needs to. At the same time she should tell him to stop phoning. You can ask her to do this because the phone is yours even if the boyfriend isn't! Should he ring thereafter, you can feel justified in ending the conversation and it's best not to have a dialogue anyway. The more you spell things out, the more he'll probably believe your daughter remains interested – it's the 'mad' part of infatuation. Three suggestions. If he's a total nuisance, ask the phone company to intercept your calls. This deters all but the most persistent. Or filter calls through an answerphone. Or try the new 'Convertaphone' which alters your voice from female to male (or male to female or adult to child) at the push of a button. (From Innovation Mail Order, Swindon SN5 8SN.)

Am I old-fashioned?

Quite recently, I asked my twenty-year-old niece Sue to stay with me and was delighted when she agreed. Then she telephoned to ask if she could bring her boyfriend too. I was about to say yes when she told me not to worry about making up an extra room because 'they'd share'. I was at a loss for words and immediately spoke to her father. His reaction amazed me. He said neither he nor my sister had any objections because their daughter was a legal adult and what she did in private was her own business. I pointed out that it wasn't in private, it was in my spare room and I had some objections. The phone call ended frostily and I am not sure what to do for the best. I am uncomfortable about providing what amounts to a love-nest for my unmarried relatives. Is it really me who is out of step? Angelica.

Answer

No, because I have received several letters on the same lines this year. I can also recall a similar problem cropping up in my own family ('Mother, they have been living together for eight years') and it is also a question I am often asked on television. However, people keep asking because there is no obvious answer. If you were the only person in the world to feel this way the matter would not be controversial. But I think society is still either uncomfortable about endorsing pre-marital sex, or in the process of changing its mind. The battle-lines also tend to be drawn between different age and religious groups.

First, let's stress that you are completely at liberty to make the rules in your own house. I wouldn't want a guest to cross my front door, light a cigarette, ask what I paid for my three-piece suite then use it to kiss and cuddle his wife. Call me old-fashioned, but that's how I feel. And we base our rules on what we feel. Second, having said that, hardly anyone under the age of 25 would get too upset to hear that a twenty-year-old girl was sleeping with her boyfriend, engaged or not, especially if she had a 'steady' relationship. They believe it happens in several branches of the Royal Family, won't frighten the horses nor draw forth the wrath of God. They may be right about that, they may not. Third, quite a few parents have arrived at the view that it's better to know where their children make love under circumstances which are secure, than to leave them to the tender mercies of public parks and the backs of battered cars. This is not to say they are eager; they find themselves evolving this philosophy against the relentless pressures of modern life. They know their children 'are going to do it'. Fourth, and I wonder if you'd find this a help in your dilemma, such parents actually ask themselves what their objections are based on? After all, being honest, many of us had pre-marital sex in the 1960s and 70s (rumour and the history books say it was occurring in the 50s and 40s). Would our lives have been easier if our families had been more understanding and accommodating? Do we simply censure on a hand-me-down basis through the generations without questioning our belief? So grill your feelings: 'Will anything truly terrible happen if 1) this young couple share a bed; 2) they are sexual in it, and 3) the bed happens to be one of mine?' If your answer is still yes, then confidently explain to your niece what the sleeping arrangements will be when she visits. You never know, she may even have been testing you.

Vibrator

My six-year-old daughter Sandra recently discovered my vibrator lying on the bed after I'd forgotten to put it away. She asked me what it was and I told her it was my massager. She seemed to accept this but later asked my mother-in-law whether she'd got one too – 'You know, Granny, the big one like a policeman's truncheon?' My mother-in-law is so shocked she won't talk to me. How do I convince her I'm not a bad parent? Susan.

Answer

By continuing to build on your excellent relationship with Sandra and by *not* being too shocked to talk to her granny. From time to time children inevitably land us in the manure but you know you've done nothing wrong. You enjoy vibro-massage, have probably done so for years and probably plan to continue – because it makes you feel wonderfully relaxed. That's your story and you're sticking to it. On the question of massage, show Granny you haven't a disapproving bone in your body – just as she has her private life so you have yours. Then change the subject.

Comic problems

I've just read one of my daughter's comics which seems to be full of what I can only call unhealthy romance. As the mother of three girls aged ten, ten and eight, I am horrified to find it's now considered normal for nine-year-olds to have 'boyfriends', at least in any other context than that of a purely innocent relationship. Children these days seem to me to be growing up far too quickly and these magazines do no favours to those of us parents who are striving to keep our children innocent and allow them to enjoy their childhood. Do you think I was right to confiscate her magazine? Felicity.

Answer

I think that's your decision and of course we're all extremely bothered when children use adult language and behaviour at too early an age. However, I wonder whether it's the best way to protect your child? Youngsters take their cue not just from families but from television, comics, peer groups and the play-ground. Whether we like it or not, today they start thinking about having close romantic friends from approximately the age of eight upwards. Yes, eight! For contrast – I started at seventeen, my grown-up sons at fifteen, and my thirteen-year-old son began last year. However, saying 'You are too young to feel as you do' or 'We won't talk about what's actually going on' means they just tune out. They read these magazines, for instance, because the subject is given an uncensored airing. From personal as well as professional experience I appreciate how difficult it is to raise a child of either sex. However, I don't think we can say 'children are innocent' and leave it at that. First, they hear (from news programmes) about every tragedy in the modern world, from Aids to Bosnia, and ask questions which we ought to answer. Second, they are 'naturally' quite horrible to each other on numerous occasions. There's also serious evidence to show that if children are 'protected' from knowledge of the facts of life they are much more vulnerable to abuse and exploitation if it's encountered because they don't begin to understand what's going on. In other words, as parents we could take some comfort from knowing that a more streetwise child is a much safer child. If any confusions do arise, a good mum (or dad) can always be close at hand to offer extra perspective.

Girlfriends

My son is fifteen and doesn't have a girlfriend. He says this is because girls in his year will only go out with boys aged seventeen or over while girls aged thirteen to fifteen look far too immature. Is this really so? Sue.

Answer

It's generally true and always was. Girls reach puberty about two years before boys, so they look 'up' the age scale for partners rather than across or down. The situation doesn't change much till later teens. However, it's not true that fifteen-year-old boys never have girlfriends. As we all know, given a change of clothes, many fourteen-year-old girls easily pass for eighteen or twenty and would easily make a mature-looking partner for your son. So what you're really hearing is 'I need a bit of encouragement, mum, please.'

Gay son

We're a very happily married couple with four lovely children but our world fell apart when one of our sons, who is 23 years old, told us he is gay. We are finding it very difficult to come to terms with as we were so very proud of him. He has told us he'd like to bring his boyfriend of six months for a meal. Please help us to come to understand and accept this situation. Mr and Mrs X.

Answer

I'm glad you are able to write with an open mind even though your distress is obvious. So many parents get stuck in an aggressive prejudice or lose themselves in self-recrimination – 'It's all our fault!' – when a little common sense would serve much better. Unless we've got our heads stuck in the sand we all know that homosexuality is quite common. Even if you've never spoken to a gay person, you've got friends who have or you've seen someone on TV – a famous footballer, actor, skater, politician, journalist, tennis ace – who is known to be 'out'. (Of the secret homosexuals, perhaps the most startling recent revelations concern the long-term head of the FBI, J Edgar Hoover, who was a camp transvestite at home). Nor is there a clear general pattern showing why some individuals end up loving their own sex. No respectable genetic or psychological evidence points a finger – the fact is we don't know what makes us heterosexual, let alone what makes other people different or bisexual. So please clear your mind of 'self-blame' – it's nothing you did! Then you have to face the heart of the difficulty. Even though prejudice is unacceptable there is still a problem of acceptance and adjustment. It isn't good enough to chant, 'Homosexuality is a normal way of life for x per cent of the population in every society throughout history.' The fact is you weren't ready for this and you must experience grief because of it. This is unavoidable when you feel your world has fallen apart. The grief starts with shock – 'we had no idea' – and you feel foolish. Then you worry about what the family and neighbours will think. In your head, you run through all the awkward explanations you will have to give. Above all you feel bereft of grandchildren from your

boy. Then you worry for his life as you open the paper
and read yet another story about HIV ... I suggest that
you as parents discuss all these depressing aspects *first*.
Not with your son – he doesn't need to hear it – but
between yourselves. Shed a tear if you want and count
your losses. It's only when you've felt all the negative
feelings that your heart will allow you to appreciate
other viewpoints. Then the transformation can be
utterly healing. For example, this is still the same son
you've loved all these years – he hasn't suddenly
acquired three heads. He trusts you enough to tell you
his difficult secret and he wants you to go on knowing
and loving him. He may never become a father but you
cannot be certain he would have done so anyway. His
career shouldn't be affected – if anything, gay men end
up richer and more successful than those who have to
pay for families and run the gauntlet of divorce! As for
HIV – the message is that gay people are nowadays
more careful than the rest of us even though we all need
to take precautions. Please agree to the dinner then take
it one day at a time. You could boost your confidence by
contacting Acceptance, an organization for parents who
share your predicament (tel 0795 661463).

Daughter banned from boyfriend

Our family is extrovert but my fifteen-year-old daughter
Pauline has just been banned from her boyfriend's
house for always hugging and kissing him. Are we at
fault? Carrie.

Answewr

We never like it when neighbours or another family
appear to 'criticize' our manners or morals. It raises lots
of issues to do with 'authority' and makes us remember

being 'told off' when young. It also raises the sensitive question of what is sexually acceptable nowadays (answers on a postcard, please). I can see that this episode would undermine the confidence of both you and your daughter. However, it is invaluable to be able to use touch to express feelings so never regret teaching your daughter this lesson. At the same time, she has just learned that not everyone can tolerate the same degree of openness. It might have been a good idea to warn her more strongly that 'different folks have different rules for strokes', whether in public or private. All the same, it won't kill her to absorb this information today. Don't pry, but see if you've heard all the facts. Did things actually go a bit further than you've been told? Make the boyfriend especially welcome in your home to express your continued support (and to avoid forcing them to sample the romantic pleasures of the local football park after dark). Allow a cooling-off period to pass before suggesting his parents are approached. See if it's acceptable that you have the first chat with 'the other side'. Negotiate a new understanding between the families after you have patiently listened to their complaints and/or outrage. Finally, ensure your daughter knows how and where to get information on contraception.

Daughter's first love

My fourteen-year-old daughter Naomi has fallen in love with her best friend's brother. She hasn't talked to him much but is obviously very attracted. The problem is that her best friend keeps teasing her about it. She says things like 'Go on, you fancy him, don't you?', especially when her brother is in the room. Naomi comes home embarrassed and distressed and I don't know what to advise for the best. Corina.

Answer

First, let me give you full marks for not adding to Naomi's troubles. She obviously has a good relationship with you. Too many parents squash their children's early romantic attachments under a heap of destructive criticism. Second, Naomi not only has to cope with the 'how to talk to him' problem, which any woman of any age has to face with a desirable male. She has to do this for the first time. In other words, the pressure is really on. She hasn't got successful memories to fall back on. It can seem like she's at the mercy of public opinion. Therefore, encourage her to feel pleased with her passion rather than threatened by it. She has lots of room for manoeuvre with you on her side. Tell Naomi she's being teased for two common reasons. The first is jealousy – maybe her friend wants Naomi to herself. The second is because it's awkward for this friend suddenly to see her brother as a pin-up. She probably knows him better as the nuisance who used to make mud pies and torture spiders. Suggest she replies to her best friend boldly, 'Yes, you're right! I do like your brother.' After all, there's nothing abnormal in liking people, is there? Even her best friend may one day want a fella. When the air is cleared, maybe Naomi could offer her friend reassurance and ask for help: 'I really want to stay friends with you, but tell me how best to get to know your brother.' Invite brother and sister round for food, or a trip out. Don't play matchmaker. Who knows whether this boy is remotely interested in Naomi? Your job is just to supply enough confidence for Naomi to find out.

We circumcised our son

When my son was a baby we had him circumcised. This was not for any religious reason but because the doctor in the hospital recommended it. Also my own husband is circumcised. Now my boy is fourteen and wants to know why we did this? He says he feels deformed and will never forgive us. I feel very guilty. Patricia.

Answer

It can be very difficult to justify an action which is no longer fashionable so I can sympathize with your feelings. However, I would point out that fourteen-year-old boys have a knack of making their parents feel guilty whatever the status of their private parts. One great psychologist said the place of parents was always in the wrong. Be that as it may, you can't put your son's foreskin back. The best you can manage is an emotional damage-limitation exercise. Explain to your son why you thought this operation was a good thing fourteen years ago. You did it to help not hurt. Be patient but don't grovel. Let him be angry if he wants. Concede you might not put him through the same ritual if he were born today but ideas do change. Tell him that millions of men in the USA and Europe, including his father, have experienced a non-religious circumcision with no ill effects whatsoever. Say that many women prefer the circumcised condition for reasons of both appearance and hygiene. Reassure him that sex will work properly. This is not like female 'circumcision' which destroys sexual ability. Add that circumcisions are often carried out for medical reasons too, even on adults, so it carries no sense of stigma.

Some useful telephone numbers
and addresses

The Brook Advisory Service: central office 071-708
1234/1390; 24-hour automated helpline 071-410 0420
The Family Planning Association, 27-35 Mortimer
Street, London W1N 7RJ. Telephone: 071-636 7866
National Society for Prevention of Cruelty to Children's
Child Protection Helpline (free): 0800 800 500
Childline (free): 0800 1111 (You can also write to them:
Freepost 1111, London N1 OBR)
Kidscape: 071-730 3300
Family Matters: 0474 537392
Asian Family Counselling: 081-997 5749